THE GAME
Winning by Virtue
One Move at A Time™

Her Royal Majesty
Princess Merrilee of Solana

R. Merrilee

Published by EDK Books and
Distributed by EDK Distribution, LLC
edkbooksanddistribution.com
edkbooksanddistribution@gmail.com | (206) 227-8179

The Game - Winning by Virtue One Move at A Time™
Copyright © 2023 by Princess Merrilee of Solana®©™

DISCLAIMER: The author is not a medical professional, licensed psychologist, or specialist healthcare professional. The philosophy provided in this book is not intended to replace healthcare, medical, nutritional therapy, psychotherapy services or attempts to diagnose, treat, prevent, cure any physical, mental, or emotional issue by the care of healthcare or other psychological professionals.

ISBN: 978-0-956065-11-4

Library of Congress Control Number: 2023901146

Kingdom of Terathea Registration Number: 11559600000000000.1

Printed in the United States of America

10 9 8 7 6 5 4 3 2 1

This book is written expressly for the library of the Author

Cover design-book layout: Julie K. Lee @ Lee Creative

The moment we were introduced, I knew she was the one.
Her frequency and vibration
told me that this is the tree of life.
Queen Merrilee is the Lady of Love.

Aroha-nui. Agape Love always.

Ariki-nui-Kawenata: Marsich-Crown-Kingdom:
The Kingdom House of IO

No eye has seen, no ear has heard,
no mind has conceived,
what God has prepared for those who love him.

1 Corinthians 2:9

TABLE OF CONTENTS

Dedication

The word and instruction is Divine in Holy Spirit.
All Glory Be to God.

FOREWORD

Excerpt from the book Knowing Merrilee, by Craig Lipscomb

It's not every day that we get the opportunity to come into contact with royalty. In my case, that's never happened quite the way I'm about to describe in this book. Now, you may be wondering why this book even needs an introduction, but when it comes to Her Royal Majesty, Princess Merrilee, it's better to give an introduction.

Introductions give people time to prepare for a speaker or an event. You can sit down, pause your thoughts, and mentally get ready for something unexpected, something particularly spectacular, someone who will rock the foundation of belief, identity, and purpose within the first ten minutes of any real conversation—not intentionally, but because of who she is.

Her message is simple: she's here to teach people how to love. Which seems simple enough at first, because we all want that. We all think we know some version of love. From what we've shared with parents, children, lovers, and friends, we coin this term 'love,' thinking that we know what it is and how to offer it to the people important in our lives.

But when face-to-face with someone who really knows how to love, and embodies that, we come face-to-face with a moment of truth. The self-realization of being in front of someone who challenges you to bare your heart in ways that expose everything sensitive about your past, present, and future has an arresting effect, and definitely requires an introduction.

This introduction is just to give you a moment to sit down and reflect on meeting someone who commands the pomp and circumstance of a true arrival, because when the Queen arrives, it's too late to study how best to show up. This book is about how I, thankfully, had the pleasure of coming face-to-face with that moment of truth, and rather than choosing to prove how much I thought I knew; I did something quite different—something I recommend you do as well—just listen.

The Game is a collection of everything there is to know about unconditional love wrapped up in a way to apply it to the people in your world every day; and when played correctly, it allows whoever is playing with you the opportunity to know that they're safe, loved, and respected with every word spoken, every act committed, and every thought to be had. When someone knows and feels like they can trust you like that with everything they are and everything they have, the world becomes a very different place.

I have friendships now with people that I can trust my children and their future with, my money and my belongings with, my dreams and my history with. It's really uncanny, and I look for more of those types of friendships without reservation or hesitation because it's an amazing thing to have.

I think being responsible for what happens with The Game really shows us how to love another person. The Game doesn't remove our consequences or prevent them, it teaches us how to become the kind of person who doesn't have to worry about them. So, when we do find someone that we want to love, we can, completely unhindered.

The Game is best described as life. Every choice we make is dependent on how we interact with the environment and the people in it. By addressing how I make choices with the people and things in any environment at any given time, I can incur favor or consequence based on my actions, thoughts, and words. Merrilee taught me to see the world as if all of these choices, actions, and thoughts will create a vibration in the air particles around me. She calls it the "energy field" and it's always responding to us…Always watching…Always listening to what we're doing. Because she's the teacher of this, I hear her voice behind it—it's like her voice is the energy field, because she's been teaching me how to listen to myself and to interact with this environment moment-to-moment.

In case the metaphysical escapes you, I'll reword that to simply say, how we treat people matters—including the way we treat ourselves. When we think lowly of ourselves, and treat ourselves like an afterthought (unimportant, etc.), the universe responds to that. When we think positively, and treat ourselves as royalty, purposeful, and loving, the universe responds to that too.

"Game over" is a very real thing. I've seen people actually attempt to take her concept and push it off as their own, selling it by way of media. I'm not going to say people are stupid, but I've met smarter chair legs.

Remember, as of the moment you read the words—whether here in my book or in The Game—you're responsible for it. You can't unsee it, and it will always be in play with everyone you speak to or interact with from the moment you understand it. Be careful with your answer, you are now in play...

Anyone then who knows the good he ought to do,
and doesn't do it, sins.

James 4:17

Merrilee gives humanity the obvious key to "the hard problem."
How does consciousness relate in day-to-day life?
A strong case for expanding our thinking with a
painfully simple answer...

John LaCasse

Author of Fight for the Quantum: Essays on Spirituality and Science;
After Your Children Die: Finding Yourself in the 4th Dimension;
Internatioal Baccalaureate: Effectiveness of Transcendental Teaching Styles

INTRODUCTION

When we look closely at the human condition, the origin of the problem lies in the individual's inability to know the correct response to solve the issue he himself has created. Although we might believe that we are innocent to the problem, upon closer examination we must be accountable as we are the creators of our own reality.

The solution to the problem is in the Word. Clearly, humanity has failed to fully understand the immense power held in the instruction. As God's children, we have been instructed to love and love only. The whole purpose of man is to wear the full armor of God. God is love. When we choose to love some of the time, we leave ourselves open and vulnerable to the destruction caused by the ego. The ego, if not trained, magnifies chaos and destruction.

Chaos and destruction are the result of Free Will as God has given us the option to love or not to love. Each time we choose to behave contrary to love, our problems multiply and worsen, leaving us with dis-ease. To choose love is to communicate effectively by virtue, using the power of love through purposeful intention. When we focus our intention on a loving behavior all of the time, the results exceed our greatest imagination.

The question becomes, how do we choose love all of the time? The Game gives clear and simple instruction. The Game demands purposeful attention to our behavior, giving us cause to slow down and think before responding. What you are about to experience is a formula to simplify the complexity of love by aligning your left brain of logic and reason with your right brain of creative expression.

Men tend to lean on logic and reason where women tend to lean on creative expression.

To understand one another, The Game requires us to use both left and right brain in order to stay in play. The result is effective communication. Effective communication helps us to foster rich and rewarding lifelong relationships built on honor, integrity, and virtuous behavior to maintain our most valuable treasure, trust within each other.

The value of The Game should not be reduced to romantic interaction. The formula applies to every interaction in life and will prove to be invaluable the more attention you give to its mastery.

The Purpose of Man

Of many books there is no end and too much study wearies the body.
The conclusion of the matter is this: Love your one and only God
and keep his Commandments for this is the whole duty of man.

Ecclesiastes 12:12-13

The duty of man is to love. The Game offers instruction. We begin by understanding why the world is one big pain-body, suffering by our own hands with the instruments of ignorance, dishonor, defense, arrogance, and pride. Included are examples for you to discern for yourself how we unknowingly are the cause of our own problems, pain, disappointments, and consequences. Once you see how words become arrows to the heart, the instruction begins. I encourage you to take notes, highlight, and keep this book close at hand for reference. All that you need to know is included for your success. Will you commit to saving yourself? I suppose that depends on your level of pain, your awareness of it, and your desire to experience the extraordinary. Whatever your current position or status, the instruction, when followed, is guaranteed to change your life for the better in ways you've yet to imagine. How much better? Infinitely better, as you learn to change your behavior.

God be with you,
Princess Merrilee

$Part\ 1$

THE BEGINNING

"Become one with Love."

~Princess Merrilee of Solana

I contemplate where to begin.

How do I explain how far the world has strayed away from love? The reality is heartbreaking. How do I articulate a *different perspective* using the same common and very ordinary words used to communicate our diminished perception of love? A diminished perception that most believe is correct. My aim is to precisely articulate the spiritual conversion of the meaning of "God, forgiveness, sinners, sacrifice, loving our brother, and I love you" to illuminate a more clear understanding. The task feels monumental. I trust that the message will be delivered by the Holy Spirit. I pray that you are inspired to receive the invaluable lessons shared herein. Keep in mind, the depth of what you're about to embark upon is conceptually simple yet complex in its application. I have no doubt that you will understand the words, but the many opportunities you will have to apply the correct move will often be missed if you fail to understand the proximity of the test. It is to your benefit to suspend what you think you know about love, and what you have read, been told, and experienced, to align your heart and mind with new eyes to see and ears to hear. The Game, when applied, will help you to see behaviors clearly, and help you identify what to listen for during communication. A clear map offers understanding of the problem and gives you the solution to the problem when connecting all the elements together. The Game offers a formula that never fails. Love is always the answer.

Be warned, the adversary will put up a strong fight to keep you from becoming Spiritually Enlightened. Your ego is arrogant and will dismiss what is taking place by saying, "I know." It will search to recall exceptions to the science, arguing to the contrary. The ego will tell you that you're fine and you need not commit to such a silly game. When you start to pay attention to the instruction, your ego will commend you, give false praise and comfort, alluding you to think you've got this. I can assure you that you don't, nor will you ever get it if you allow the ego to distract your committed attention to the present.

The Game offers the instruction to find your way home to love. It's the narrow path that only a few will follow. You will learn how to align your heart with your head to enter the metaphysical world of energy and vibration. Your responses will direct the energy field to respond to you favorably when played correctly or with consequence when you miss the right move. Your energetic response is constant, so it's imperative that you stay focused and aware of your next move. Each time you make an allowance for yourself or others, you are moving away from becoming love to enter the wide road of destruction. Do not betray yourself. Much like a tightrope, the path is narrow. Do not concern yourself with the behaviors of others; each has their own path to follow. Let them, do not correct them. Stay focused on entering the narrow gate, watch your step, and you will find it.

I cannot promise what you'll experience along the way, as I don't know the desires of your heart. But I can absolutely promise that you will experience what your heart desires when you commit to the instruction. God says, "Your Father knows what you need before you ask." Matthew 6:8. Believe that your desires are known. You don't have to articulate, wish, pray, or even know. It is already done. Just follow the instruction. To your absolute amazement, the great and powerful "I AM" in you will be revealed to you. Stay committed by meditating on your desire to be one with love. Be open and allow the Holy Spirit to help you hear and understand the messages from those around you.

The world will sound different. You will hear the overflow of the heart in yourself and others; revealing the pain, heartache, dysfunction, injustice, fear, excuses, and insecurity we all try to hide.

With your commitment, you will begin to understand how the rules and pieces work together to reveal information you didn't understand before. Your life becomes extraordinarily wonderful. Like a domino that causes others to fall, one virtue leads to another, showing you how to move mountains. There is nothing else with such pressing value than mastering The Game. To master The Game is to know love. To know love is to know and know that you know God.

Please give serious consideration to what I'm about to say because it's important for your success. If you waver, fail to believe, make allowances, or repudiate the truth, it will be impossible for you to experience the glory of the Kingdom of Heaven on Earth. Heaven is here now, not just a promise in the afterlife. "I AM the God of the living." Matt 22:32. It is here that you will experience joy, abundance, and protection. Just remember, "It is easier for a camel to go through the eye of a needle than for a rich man to enter the Kingdom of God." Mark 10:25. The sentiment applies to everyone who has succumbed to the material world, not just the wealthy. When our beliefs are directed by logic and reason in the material world, it is nearly impossible to cross over to an intuitive directive to love shown by the Holy Spirit.

The Holy Spirit helps us let go of the false limitations, our memories, and the material world of scarcity and competition when we're open to ignite the limitless imagination of our creator within. Let go and let God. Faith is your most valuable asset. Without faith, you'll find yourself subject to a world of fear and matter where circumstances and suffering are very real. The reality of fear and matter is an illusion or hologram created to keep your greatest power hidden within the darkness.

Following the interaction of The Game, you will gain absolute confidence each time you make a loving decision with every move you make. You will also enjoy the awareness of being able to purposefully create a beautiful life for yourself; one filled with serendipity and favor. Your diligence will result in an immense sense of gratitude for the privilege of life and living. Sound too good to be true? Maybe, but you will never know until you apply yourself.

To have faith in The Game is to suspend your reservation about the power of the instruction. Align your beliefs and behavior with the idea that love is always the answer. The stronger your fortitude, the sooner your gift inside of you will be revealed. It's the fruit of who you are and the gift you are purposed to give to others. To your amazement, your passion will be far beyond your rational understanding, beyond the world of fame and fortune. This is the part where true gratitude for the gift of life will make you feel both regretful for being so ignorant and blessed to experience what so many have lived a whole lifetime never knowing.

It's always been so simple. You need only to love to receive your treasure. Your ability to exercise your free will to love is the key that unlocks the chest holding your answers—even when you don't know the questions. Your fortune lies within you; just follow the map. It won't be easy, but I promise it'll be worth it.

Remember, life is always in play. As long as you're breathing, there are consequences and favor bestowed upon you, dependent upon your vibration. A great deal of the world's population lives without purpose or direction, ignorant to the way of love, therefore ignorant to the cause of their suffering. A blind man will continue to see nothing when the lights are turned on. Do not be a blind man. Open your eyes and receive the light. The way is clear to make your way through the darkness.

Life is heavy with heartbreak, scarcity, division, self-loathing, fear, judgment, and conjecture. It's the very reason why so many individuals are losing faith in the value of love. The darkness is overwhelming. Your Salvation comes when you honor the rules, earn your pieces, know your player, and study the plays. The more focused your attention, the more magical your life becomes. Your ability to move through obstacles easily and effortlessly brings instant results and great satisfaction. The mystery of life unfolds when you know how to purposefully respond to your circumstances with love. Much like running an obstacle course in the dark, now with the lights on, you can see where to jump, pause, duck, swing, hold on, and let go to avoid the fall. Your reward is the gift.

Now that you know what to expect, will you choose to continue to live obliviously in the dark? I don't think you would want to, but The Game is not easy. In fact, it's so difficult that many will be like the rocks on which the seeds have fallen. Some seeds will die, others will be washed away with little commitment, but for some, the seeds will take root. For those that take root, the education will prove invaluable.

When you begin to play, be careful not to assume to know the correct move as it will take patience and diligence to remove your old perceptions and understanding. You must consider the pieces and rules to test your discernment. If you don't get favorable results, you're not playing right. It's not to your benefit to think that you understand what you're doing is correct, as it only serves as an opinion until the results are in. The assumption is likely to result in a loss of your king. The instruction, if not applied with humility, a pure heart, and with the intention to become love will result in suffering. The consequence of manipulation or ill intentions will have no end. No one betrays love without serious ramifications. If you are ready to continue, there is no going back once you've read the instruction. You cannot unsee what you've been shown to see. Know that you are being watched and held accountable for your thoughts, deeds, decisions, words, and actions the same as before, but now you know better. Everything hidden will come to light. The consequence is unlimited when you can no longer claim ignorance. To not know and do is not a sin, but to know and not do is a sin. Whether ignorant or not, you are responsible. Cause and effect is a universal law. Believe or not, it makes no difference. The universe will continue to respond.

There is only one truth: love. If it's not love, it's not true. This bears repeating: If it's not love, it's not true. When the truth is in question, ask yourself, is this virtuous? If the answer is no, then it's not true. It's part of the illusion. What you're experiencing is a false perception meant to suppress your power by binding you to fear. Conversely, when you align your vision with virtue, you can say to the mountain, "Throw yourself into the sea." Your faith in a loving behavior will produce all that you desire and more. However, if you are struggling with your faith, your reservation is evidence that the darkness has consumed your mind to believe in pain and suffering. Don't be a prisoner to your fears. You can create a different reality.

The definition of truth is cause for confusion and debate, as there is much pain and suffering in the world appearing to be real. The Messiah is the truth. The Messiah is the embodiment of love. The Messiah endured pain and suffering for the world because He was love. We too will endure pain and suffering when we choose to love because the ego feels the hit.

God made a promise to raise us up from suffering if we make the Most High our dwelling. The pain and suffering caused by drama will dissipate when you implement a change in your conviction to love only. Choosing to be love must be a present moment-to-moment decision to consciously respond with virtue to elevate above the lower vibrational behaviors that cause dissension. As you become closer to love, you begin to ascend spiritually to enjoy the benefits of life offered on a whole new level. Like living in a castle in the sky, you no longer concern yourself with the drama caused by people breaking the rules. God said he would command his angels where you are concerned, to protect you from evil when you follow his commandment to love your one and only God (within you) and love your neighbor as yourself (the same God that lives in you). You can trust the universal law of reciprocity to deliver a life of drama-free abundance when you acknowledge that you are responsible for your experience. Accept the fact that nothing goes unseen by the All, it's only you who fails to see your part in the big picture. Self-love is to make self-mastery your first priority. It's a biblical order. To not love yourself first is the equivalent of self-sacrifice. Do not sacrifice the Holy Spirit within you to honor your neighbor (player) first.

With each move that you're able to keep your king on the board, you've chosen to love yourself first. Self-love will hold the boundary against breaking the rules and keep your standard of behavior elevated to the Most High. Your best life begins the moment you decide to take action to become love with The One. The Father, the unseen, unlimited vibration of pure potential is observed by sub-atomic particles referred to as the field or consciousness. The field is pure love. God is love. (1 John 4:8) There is nothing else. Love is the creator of the created. The Messiah is a pure example of the embodiment of love created by the unseen God, into the physical manifestation of consciousness. The higher you elevate your awareness about love, the more spiritually enlightened you become. The Holy Spirit is light; information and wisdom accessible through higher consciousness and intuition. The Holy Spirit is the eternal library of past, present, and future knowledge. This information is accessible within every cell of your physical body. The Holy Spirit of information gives you the power to heal, gain clarity, direction, and the ability to alter the circumstances by your thoughts, words, deeds, and imagination. The universal laws of the triune; love, the Messiah, and your counselor are always working in your favor, but your actions contrary to love create a barrier. Moving the barrier is as easy as matching the energy that creates everything. The Holy Spirit will deliver what you need when you need it. One move at a time. If you don't have what you need, it's because you don't need it yet. Be patient and love harder.

To have Patience is to have Faith. Patience is the ability to let go. Stop controlling your external world. Instead, focus on controlling your internal responses to the world. Your internal world is the higher authority to bring inequity into balance. When you've mastered your Patience by having Faith, you're on your way to self-mastery. Self-mastery is the ability to control the reaction of the ego-centered, serpent mind, to respond with an elevated, heart-centered, conscious mind. There is no greater personal empowerment than to master the power of love. Having the power to control your thoughts, behavior, and responses with purpose will unleash your unlimited potential as the creator of your destiny. No longer will you live in fear of the unknown, because your behavior will give direction to your blessing. With your dedication and commitment to a divine character, you can be confident that your gifts will be delivered as promised.

As you shift your paradigm from fear of consequence to having faith in your conviction, you become witness to the passage, "No eye has seen, no ear has heard, and no mind has conceived what God has planned for those who love him." (1 Corinthians 2:9).

$Part\ 2$

WHAT IS THE GAME?

*Enter through the narrow gate for wide is the gate and
broad is the road that leads to destruction, and many enter through it.
But small is the gate, and narrow is the road that leads to life
and only a few find it.*

Matthew 7:13-14

The Game appears to be a philosophy, but really, it's a formula for the "what, when, and how" to love on purpose. Consider the complexity of a Rubik's Cube. Life is divided by color blocks (circumstances) all misaligned. When you think you have it figured out, you realize only one circumstance has been aligned. Most people don't have the patience to figure out the puzzle, or the answer to all of their circumstances. Instead, they accept the chaos. A Rubik's Cube represents a problem that can only be solved with a *formula* for the right moves leading to success. Without the formula, you will continue to play without ever reaching the solution.

To achieve the solution, reverse-engineer the problem. Consider how the misaligned, twisted cube (the hard problem) is created. The whole is divided to create moving parts (egos), multiple colors (circumstance) are applied to create complexity and confusion. The solution then, is to simplify the hard problem by removing the colors (circumstances) to see only the moving parts (humanity) without confusion. What remains are the segments (people). When you join the segments (removing the idea of separation), you find the simplicity of the

9

complete cube. That complete cube represents love. Love is the solution to the problem.

Love is the answer to align your circumstances. Your behavior toward the problem is like the Rubik's Cube; keep twisting until you have only virtue to become whole in love. Wouldn't it be helpful to know the combination to twist the Rubik's Cube into alignment on the first try? Just like the cube, the combination to love begins to have a clear path the more focused you are on learning how to play The Game. No matter what your question, concern, dilemma, or circumstance, knowing *how* to respond in love is always the right move. With each move, you gain a deeper understanding about the complexity of each virtue and how it affects the other pieces. The more complex your level of understanding, the easier The Game is to play as you learn to eliminate behaviors contrary to love.

A committed player seeks to know his player then recognize his player in himself. It's good to remember that each player will make the decision to honor *one* of two paths in life: love or money. It will become more evident with each move. The way to discern their position is to divide their actions between the rules and the pieces. Those who break the rules, by default, honor money, a fear-based reality. Those who honor money will be self-defeating and will ultimately be the cause of their own heartache, both personally and professionally. Be careful to accept what you see the first time you recognize your player's move. It will be either a rule or a virtue. A player cannot honor both love and money, you cannot play virtuous while breaking the rules.

There is no exception, no walking the line, or switching between the two. Use discernment to *identify character*. People show you who they are when they sacrifice the relationship by breaking the rules to support their fear; conversely, in love, they will sacrifice their fear to preserve the relationship. Always look to align with people who value relationships before money (fear).

Awareness and discernment about love is the armor of God. Favor is the result of knowing what love is and what love is not. Those who invest the time to polish their Game will gain respect while inspiring others to level up. Be the gift, live by example. The result of your example will leave a legacy and provide the path for your joy and happiness.

Unfortunately, the world has been programmed to honor the pursuit of money, believing in hard work, competition, and scarcity. You are not here to be weak, powerless, sick, worried, broke, helpless, and obedient to an oppressive system. You are not here to sacrifice your God-given gift in exchange for slave labor in order to survive. Now is the time to redirect your focus on the ways of love to experience your birthright.

It is by your own free will that you focus your energy and attention toward building your Board of Virtues or continue chasing the illusion of success. Your one right move will bring the unlimited and unexplained serendipity that's waiting for you to experience heaven on earth. Now is the time to recognize the absence of virtue within yourself and others. True and consistent happiness is achieved by disciplining your behavior to gain favorable responses. It is by one's own will and conviction to self-reflect, and to question assumptions, barriers, limited beliefs and expectations, logic and reason, reactions and responses.

With your commitment to understand how you respond, you will gain an unshakable confidence in who you are, where you come from, and what you are here to do.

What is The Game? The Game is a proven formula for self-mastery. It's our guide to Christ-like, virtuous behavior. To experience the magic, be love, honor the rules, gaining virtue, and forever keeping your King on the board as in a game of chess. You'll want to master The Game because your success depends upon the relationships you keep. Without the self-awareness skills necessary to play, you're subject to self-sabotage. The Game shows us the way to elevate to Christ Consciousness. The direction will be the most challenging test of self-control, self-awareness, accountability, self-love, perseverance, boundaries, ethics, and standards. Your spiritual elevation depends on your commitment to self-discipline. If you want to change the course of your reality, apply the instruction. If you want to find out how you are the creator of your life, responsible for all your blessings and favor, master The Game and you'll know your answer.

You may have doubts to the validity of this promise; be careful, your belief becomes your reality. Whether you choose to learn or disregard, The Game remains the same. Those who choose to devote themselves to learning how to play will experience a most profound sense of gratitude for the gift. You will no longer dread the day or days to come, struggling through life not knowing your purpose or where you'll end up. Gone are the worries of tomorrow. Instead, you will wake with excitement, knowing there's a gift waiting just for you when you're able to make the right move. You know the answer is love, but it's up to you to know your next move. As you become a master, no circumstance will ever prove to be your match.

Imagine knowing what to say, how to say it, and when. You no longer struggle to understand the hearts of others or wonder if your behavior will be understood. The Game is your teacher, helping you to be the best I AM for yourself and others. It's your magic wand to lift the darkness that's plagued your garden.

Should you have the tenacity, devoting your attention to unraveling its complexity, the rewards will stimulate your curiosity and determination to experience more. You'll come to understand just how limited you are in your thinking, and why it's been so difficult to experience your life to the extent of the unlimited. Your imagination is your only barrier as you come to discover your world is all about your belief and behavior.

What will you do when you realize your behavior is the secret to do, be and have anything you can dream and believe? Should you have the courage and commitment to follow the instruction, you will undoubtedly find yourself happy for the rest of your life.

$Part\ 3$

THE OBJECT OF THE GAME

The object of The Game is to rid yourself of ego-based behavior to elevate to the pureness of love; Christ Consciousness. To reach self-mastery is to unconsciously move only your pieces with every player, circumstance, challenge, and fear. The result will provide evidence of an impeccable character that will undoubtedly be blessed with favor. As promised.

No eye has seen
No ear has heard
No mind has conceived
What God has prepared for those who love him

1 Corinthians 2:9

Part 4

KARMA; CAUSE AND EFFECT

The stories shared here are not of my experience but rather they were provided by the Holy Spirit to give evidence of the ignorance in human behavior. My emotional response at the time of writing leaves no question; they are true somewhere in our existence.

You Sound Like Your Mother

In the beginning, we fell in love. Life was simple as we enjoyed each other without care or responsibility for the future. We made a commitment "to forever" as we said, "I do." Life got harder when the baby came along. Now, we're tired with not much time to dream and play like we used to. Before long, there's baby number two. The responsibility is heavy as there are bills to pay and children to raise. The days get long, and the nights are shorter; we rarely make love, and it seems we fight about everything. I hate my job, which makes things worse. How do we get back to feeling like we did when we first fell in love? The kids are growing, and now I'm noticing you sound just like your mother. I try to explain, but it goes something like this...

"Where were you? I've been waiting for you to join me for dinner."

"I had to work late."

"Then why didn't you call? Who were you with, was it that woman I saw?"

"What are you talking about? I never even talk to her."

"Don't lie to me, I saw your phone."

"Why are you looking at my phone? Besides, she only called me once."

"Why didn't you tell me? What do you have to hide?"

"I don't have anything to hide. I just didn't think it was a big deal."

"Oh really, how would you feel if you saw a text from a man on my phone?"

"Why do you ask? Do you have a text on your phone I don't know about?"

"No, I'm asking you."

"Yeah, but why? Maybe you're the one with a guilty conscience, and that's why you're paranoid and projecting onto me."

"I'm not paranoid. If you want another woman, she can have you."

"Oh, is that right? So now you don't care about me?"

"Well, you don't seem to care about me, if you did you wouldn't be seeing other women."

"Seeing other women? I'm not seeing other women! Besides, if I were, I wouldn't be so stupid to leave a text on my phone for you to see."

"Oh, that's great! Thanks, thanks for that!" (She leaves crying).

Dad's Authority

We love our children so much. They are the center of our world, with all their giggles, cries, cuddles, cozy pajamas, and need of our attention. They are our pride and joy as everything they do reflects our awesome creation. Little did we know, they would also be the magnifying glass of our dysfunction. Once a bundle of joy, this tiny person has now become a dividing chasm, showing us the difference in our way of parenting. I say no, she says yes, while our child learns how to manipulate.

"Go to your room, Johnny. Your dad and I need to talk." Johnny is on the other side of the door listening to all that's going on, feeling he's to blame. The tears run down his face as he listens to his mother yell at his father.

"Why do you keep saying 'no' before you talk with me?"

"I have a right to say 'no.' He's my child too."

"It's not about him being your child. You're exercising your authority for no good reason."

"What do you mean, 'no good reason'? I am the man of the house, and what I say goes."

"Oh, so I don't have a say because I'm a woman?"

"No, I'm just saying you should honor my decision."

"And if that decision doesn't make sense, I have to go with it?"

"It does make sense, just not to you."

"What am I, stupid?"

"I can understand what you're saying, and I can understand about the importance of your decision, but this is nonsense, and I won't have it."

"You won't have it? What are you going to do, leave?"

"How dare you say that to me! Do you really think I wouldn't leave?"

"If you want to, then do it."

"I didn't say I wanted to."

"Then, don't threaten to leave."

"I didn't threaten, you tested me!"

"I tested you? Come on, you're ridiculous, just like your mother."

My Best Friend Danny

I grew up in a household where my parents always fought about something. I never felt comfortable inviting my friends over for fear of being embarrassed. Most times, I would come home from school and go straight to my room. My mom would make dinner, and Dad would come home from work tired with not much to say. I never really knew my dad; he always just asked about my homework and shuffled me off to bed. Alone in my room, I wished I had someone to talk to, someone who cared. Every day was the same, nothing of interest or anything to learn. I just felt so bored with my life. The kids at school wanted to hang out and talk about sex, but I never fit in. My mom tried her best to be there for me, volunteering at school, baking cookies, and things. Thank goodness for my best friend Danny up the street. We got together and did fun stuff like play games. Neither of us really knew what we were doing; we told stories of what life would be like if things were different. We were best friends until Matt came along. Matt and Danny would hang out without me. Then one day, Matt came over to visit. We hung out and it was okay until he started to talk about Danny in a way that made me feel uneasy.

"Hey, have you talked to Danny lately?"

"No, about what?"

"Oh, I don't know. He was mad the other day and mentioned something about you copying his homework."

"What? I never copy his homework."

"Really? He said you asked him for help with your math, then took his homework and copied it."

"That's not true. He's not even good at math. Why would I ask for his help?"

"I'm not sure, but I don't think he wants to be friends with you anymore."

"What? I'm calling him right now!"

"Hello, Danny? Why did you tell Matt you didn't want to be my friend anymore?"

"What, when did I say that?"

"You told him I copied your math homework and that you didn't want to be friends."

"No, I didn't."

"Really? Why would Matt lie to me about it?"

"I don't know. Why would you believe him over me?"

"Because you guys are hanging out all the time and we're not."

"That's because you don't want to."

"Says who? You're the one who goes straight home after school every day."

"What does that mean?"

"I just figured you didn't want to hang out."

"Never mind. I'll talk to you later."

The Prettiest Girl in the Room

My brother and I had the perfect parents. My mother adored me. Everywhere we went, she would brag to her friends about all my accomplishments and buy me all my favorite things when we went shopping. She would always tell me how I was the prettiest girl in the room anywhere we went. My dad and brother hung out a lot, just like me and mom. We would go shopping, and they would do guy stuff. Later, when we got home, I helped Mom in the kitchen while Dad and my brother watched TV. At bedtime, my mom laid with me until I fell asleep. I pretended to be awake whenever she tried to leave so she would stay.

This went on for years until I began to realize that maybe she didn't want to go back to bed. She and my dad were always so busy with my brother and me that I hadn't noticed the distance between them. My brother and I eventually left home. I fell in love with my husband after meeting him through a mutual friend. He was so handsome, all the girls liked him, but he liked me because I was the prettiest girl in the room. Everything seemed to be perfect as we both fell in love at first sight. Soon after, we were married. The first few years were great as we worked together to create a home and get our careers off the ground. We had a routine each morning. He made the …and I made the bed. We would kiss and be off to work. In the evening, we'd watch our favorite show after dinner, and then call it a night. The sex was good and would often end with a kiss and roll over. The distance between us grew without notice.

It hadn't become obvious until a colleague, Patrick, started to notice me. Every day, Patrick complimented me on my hair or what I was wearing. Then, he would do sweet things like buy me a coffee and leave it at my desk. Soon, I found myself looking forward to seeing him, wondering what he would say or do. The contrast with my husband became more obvious as I realized he never gave me compliments or bought me sweet things. One night I asked, "Do you love me?"

"What? Of course, I love you. Why would you ask that?"

"I don't know, never mind."

I knew he loved me. What else could he say? Still, the emptiness of something missing was there. At work, Patrick continued to be kind and considerate of me. I felt myself begin to gravitate toward him. My husband must have felt something was different.

"Are you okay?"

"Yes."

"Are you sure?"

"Yes."

What could I say at this point? He wouldn't understand. It was best to keep my mouth shut. It wasn't long after that he asked me again.

"Are you okay?"

"I don't know."

"What do you mean you don't know, what's wrong? You've been distant for a long time now. Are you happy?"

"Yeah, I'm happy."

"You don't seem to be happy. Is there something I did?"

"No, you didn't do anything."

"Well okay, but you're not making me happy."

"I'm not making you happy—what's that supposed to mean?"

"I don't like seeing you like this, and you won't tell me what's wrong. So, how can I fix it?"

"How do you know you can fix it?"

"I don't, but at least let me give it a try."

"I don't feel that you love me."

"What?! That's what this is all about? I told you, of course I love you. Why are you questioning me?"

"Because you don't tell me I'm pretty or do sweet things for me."

"Are you serious right now? Why are you being so needy? Wait, is it that time of the month for you?"

"I'm serious, please don't make this about hormones."

"I'm sorry, but I come home every night, there's a roof over your head, we make love…"

"We make love?"

"Yes! We make love!"

"I don't think so."

"Oh my gosh, what are you saying?"

"I'm saying it feels more like sex."

"Whatever! You're the only woman I'm having sex with, okay?"

"I don't want to have sex. I want to make love and hear you tell me I'm beautiful!"

"You are beautiful, dammit!"

"I don't believe you."

"What?"

"I gotta go to bed. Let's talk about this tomorrow."

I don't know why I didn't end my marriage right then; I suppose I thought it would get better. Instead, I had an affair with Patrick, and after fifteen years in a loveless marriage, we finally called it quits.

My Niece Jada

I grew up in the church. My parents took my sisters and me every Sunday. My mom was active with fundraisers and bake sales. My sister, Carolyn, was the singer in the family. She had a beautiful voice; everyone complimented her after the sermon. I loved the lunch get-togethers, listening to all the stories shared about families and adventures. The pastor was well-respected among the community; he and Carolyn were very close. When Carolyn was introduced to John, her husband, through a church member, pastor Bob performed the ceremony. As pastor of the church for forty years, he also baptized their four children.

I remember it was the summer before his last year of service that my nine-year-old niece, Jada, told me about Pastor Bob. He had been molesting her since she was five. Jada was too afraid to tell my sister. I was devastated. All those years, my sister trusted him as he escorted Jada away. He took to her as his favorite, never giving special attention to the others. Thinking back, I remember him frequently asking her for a kiss on the cheek while sitting her on his lap. I didn't know what to do first: call the authorities, call him to give him a piece of my mind, or tell my sister. I decided my sister needed to know first. I didn't know how to start, as I knew the news would break her heart on so many levels.

"Carolyn, we need to talk."

"Okay?"

"I'll be right over."

As I drove to my sister's house, the pit of my stomach was in knots thinking about the years of abuse my niece was subject to in plain sight. The guilt of not knowing and not being able to help her was more than I could take. When I finally reached Carolyn's house, I was crying.

"What's the matter, hon? Come in, sit down."

I was sobbing. I couldn't control my emotions long enough to get a word out. Carolyn knew this was serious and became afraid.

"Honey, you're scaring me. Please tell me what it is."

With just enough air to choke out one word, all I could say was Jada's name. That was enough to send her into a panic; she immediately started screaming for Jada.

"Shhh, she's here. Please," I begged through the tears, "just give me a minute."

My sister started to get angry and impatient. I knew I had to say something and say it delicately.

"Carolyn, Jada… our Jadie girl…was molested." I started to cry again while my sister asked questions half-angry and half-confused, demanding answers. "It was Pastor Bob."

"What?! NOoooooo…" she started to scream and cry at the same time.

"NOoooo, how… when? What? Jada!" In a panicked voice, she yelled, "Jadie girl, come down here please."

"Please, Carolyn, don't take it out on her. She was afraid to tell you." I tried my best to dry my tears and hold it together for Jada while my sister, in denial, looked for answers.

"Jada, what have you been telling your aunt?" She looked at me disappointed, as if I were supposed to keep her secret. I just shook my head and whispered, "I had to, Jada."

"Why didn't you tell me, Jada?" The little girl looked at her mom with a blank stare.

"Are you sure? Tell me what he did to you. Don't be making up stories about Pastor Bob. This is a very serious accusation. Did he touch you?" Jada nodded with her head down, as if she were to blame.

"Jada, this is going to hurt Pastor Bob if you're not telling the truth." Jada looked up with complete despair as her mother questioned the truth.

"Carolyn, we have to go to the authorities. We have to report him as soon as possible."

My sister stopped in a moment of contemplation and said, "I will talk with him tomorrow."

I couldn't believe what I was hearing. "Talk to him about what? What can he possibly say to correct what has been done?"

She looked at me with that authoritative stare.

"What will the church think? I can't let this get out. It'll ruin our family, his reputation, and Jada will be the talk of the town. I think we should settle this quietly and respectfully."

"Respectfully?!" I didn't want to fight in front of Jada to make matters worse, but I couldn't help but reiterate the absurdity.

"Jada honey," I took her in my arms and hugged her.

"It's going to be okay. You did the right thing."

The Only Child

I was an only child raised by parents who never had time for me. For eighteen years, I did what I had to do to get through school and stay out of trouble. It wouldn't have mattered much; my parents were both career-minded and successful. I always had a nanny or someone to take care of me while they took business trips, both together and separately. They never would have noticed anything different. From the outside, my life appeared to be charmed. I went to the best schools, I had fine clothes, and always had people with me—just not my parents. The only time we were together, it seemed, were business affairs when they entertained important people, and I was there to represent. I didn't know my parents aside from their professional persona. My mom wasn't one to bake cookies or ask me how my day was. A kiss and hug in passing was the norm as she headed off to somewhere. My dad was pretty important. I wish he would have spent more time sharing about what he did exactly. Other than his title, I never really knew what he did from day-to-day. Our relationship was more proper, as he informed me of his standards and expected me to meet them. Needless to say, there wasn't a lot of love from the home front. When I turned eighteen, I decided to leave home and join the army. I didn't know what to expect, but the idea of having brothers and sisters sounded good to me. I wanted to belong; I wanted a family. When it was time to say goodbye, my mother had a meeting she needed to get to. I don't think she had the mental space to accept my leaving; her last words to me were, "I love you, son. I'll see you when you get back." My dad was clearly disappointed, as he had plans for me to work for the company. He struggled to execute the proper sentiment because his plan was unexpectedly thwarted. He shook my hand and said, "You're a man now, son." I picked up my belongings and left. Three months later, I was stationed in the Gulf War. I knew I would never make it home, and I didn't.

Rusty

How did I get here? One minute, I was just a kid having fun, going to school with my boyfriend, and the next minute, I was pregnant, alone, and scared. My parents were supportive, but my boyfriend wanted me to abort the baby. I couldn't do it. He gave me an ultimatum. So, I left him. Ten years later it's me, my son and his precious little cockapoo, Rusty. We found Rusty in a box on the side of the road with a sign that said, "Free to good home." I knew better than to go look in that box, but as soon as we did, this adorable reddish brown, curly-haired puppy started to whine, 'take me home.' It was love at first sight for Robby. "Can we have him, Mom? Can we have him, please?"

I loved the sight of that dog too. I knew they would be best friends, and they were. They took to each other like twins. Robby loved Rusty. It wasn't too long after that I met Paul. He was tall and fairly handsome, and I hadn't dated in a while, so I thought I would take a chance. We got along well, and Robby and Rusty didn't mind either. It seemed we were becoming a family. Paul and I took Robby and Rusty out to the park and we would watch them for a couple hours until it was time to go.

Paul was a factory worker who didn't care for his job or the people he worked with. I heard stories about the people who would make him so angry. Sometimes, he got angry all over again just sharing the story. It scared me. A couple of times, he was outraged and caused damage to the warehouse. I knew then, he had anger issues, but he hadn't been angry to that extreme with me directly. As time went on, we started to disagree about stupid things that I believe had more to do with someone else, but that he was taking out on me. Then, the day came where I will never forgive myself. I was in the kitchen making lunch for Robby when I heard Paul's car pull up. Robby and Rusty were playing in the garage. Paul came in with a look of anger on his face.

"What happened?"

"That fucker fired me!"

"What?"

"I went into work, and in front of everyone, he called my name out loud and told me he wanted to talk to me in his office."

"What did you do?"

"What do you mean, what did I do? I didn't do anything! Why are you blaming me for doing something when you don't even know what's going on?!"

"No, I meant, what did you do when he called you?"

"I went into his fucking office, what do you think?"

"Were people watching?"

"What the fuck kind of question is that? Of course, people were watching. I work in a damn factory, you fucking bitch! Shit! I came here to tell you about my day and all I get is shit-ass questions that make no sense!"

I watched in shock as he stormed out the door. In a moment of uncontrolled anger, Paul picked up a rock, swung it around without care and let go of it. In an instant, my life was changed forever. He missed hitting Robby, but the rock hit Rusty in the back of the head. Robby let out a blood curdling scream as his dog lay bleeding from a gash in the head, his body twitching on the floor. Paul, realizing what he had done, was even more angry knowing Rusty would die. In an instant, he gave the dog a final kick to the head to put him out of his misery. Rusty was gone. Robby, in disbelief and shock, fell to the floor and cried uncontrollably over Rusty.

"Get the hell out of here, you asshole! I can't believe you killed my dog! It could have been Robby, for God's sake!"

No amount of yelling could express my fear over what could have just happened. In an instant, I felt responsible and regret for not doing something when I had the chance. Rusty would still be here if I had just walked away. *Damn, why didn't I just walk away?* It's been six years since that day. I pressed charges for the loss of our beloved Rusty, but my beautiful, loving son hasn't said a word since the day he witnessed his best friend being kicked to his death. I'll never forgive myself. Dear God help me.

The Bag Lady

I remember when it all started. I was a typical teenager who idolized the girls on social media. I watched them do their hair and makeup and tried to do the same. I wasn't very good, but with practice I started to get the hang of it. That's when I began getting attention from boys. I liked it. I was motivated to study every movement and style, changing only a bit to create my own way. As the attention grew, so did my confidence. My courage started to take over as I became a contributor and not just a follower. Every day I watched my likes and follows increase. I was obsessed with becoming an influencer.

Pictures, pictures, and more pictures. I studied to see which ones got the most attention, and then took more. My following increased. Both men and boys were reaching out wanting my attention. Of course, I never went out with someone older than me, only the boys my age. The more attention I got, the more I craved. My social media world became my existence. Behind the scenes, I was nothing. I didn't know who I was, where I was going, or what I was doing. Like a junkie, I just needed my fix, checking my profile every hour to see who liked my picture and how many new followers I had.

When a cute boy commented on my picture, I would search through my messages to see if he messaged me then answer him back. I had a date every Friday night. It was the time of my life. Then, I met Joey. He was hot. He left me a message and we started talking. We went out on Friday night and our chemistry was amazing. I didn't want to spend time with anyone else, so every Friday we enjoyed each other. During the week, he commented on my pictures and told me how hot I was. Our cyber relationship was exciting as we flirted over public text. I wanted to be sexier and give more of what he could see but not touch. When Friday came around, it was our turn to get wild. We had sex in the car, in the theater, even in the bathroom at the restaurant. We were wild. One night, he offered me cocaine. I had never tried a drug before, but I trusted him.

It felt good and made the sex even better. I didn't realize it then, but I was addicted. Addicted to the attention, to my persona, to the wild and crazy relationship, and now to cocaine. It didn't bother me. I had it under control until my courage escalated to dangerous choices like never before. I just wanted more. I wanted more fun and more sex. Friday night lost its luster as new boys were coming around. I loved the thrill of a new ride who could supply my needs. I guess I started to change, because my parents asked questions about my frail look. The usual fullness in my breasts, that I loved to show off, wasn't there. I didn't care; it was easy to fool the camera. My pictures became more daring the higher I became. Each picture drawing a new crowd I wanted to explore.

While I had my fun, I guess I didn't realize the sacrifice I made each time I gave a piece of me in return for my junk. My parents caught on and put me in rehab, but I just bade my time knowing exactly what I wanted to do. I needed to be on top of my game, where people knew my face and my name. I wanted to live my life out of control because I lived for the thrill of it all. At least, that's what I thought. Looking back, I think of all I missed while I lived in my illusionary existence. I didn't have the typical life; I sacrificed it all. Now I'm living on the streets begging for food and my fix. The looks I get are not the same as before. I'm a bag lady with no place to go.

Every day people across the world use exchanges of words without knowing the damage they cause. There's very little understanding of the destruction that flows from their mouths, caused by the overflow of their hearts. Each player takes the hit, holds it in as best they can to protect the ego then explodes when the time is right. Around and around, we go, changing partners like a square dance; hoping the next will be the right one. The environment is irrelevant. No matter the background, region, race or diversity, most people show up already hurt, insecure, afraid, and with only their ego and pride left to defend.

The Messiah said, "Follow me," and somehow, we the people misinterpreted that to mean worshipping someone or something outside of ourselves. Many believe they need to know his stories, and preach the gospel, but conveniently dismiss being accountable for their behavior. From the time of his story, humanity has lost their belief that he will keep his promise to fulfill our dreams. How easily we have forgotten that our only purpose in this human experience is to find our way back to love, so we may experience the delivery of his promise. Love is the answer. Love is the way to create harmony within oneself, with each other, and the way to create a life of incredible abundance, joy, and fulfillment doing exactly what you love to do.

The Game is the remedy to our ignorance. I'll describe The Game, and how you'll go about playing, by adopting the principles and applying them effectively in an easy to understand formula.

$Part\ 5$

WHY LEARN?

The fear of the Lord is the beginning of knowledge,
but fools despise wisdom and instruction.

Proverbs 1:7

Aside from our original manual, The Game helps us attain wisdom and understanding when we follow the instruction. Our life experience changes from living by trial and error, to having present-moment awareness with each other. When we have present-moment awareness, we make better decisions for our greatest success because it enables us to recognize what is important, who is important now, and where love is and is not. Although the Bible gives us direction, had the instruction been clear, we would all be on the same page about how to love each other to access our greatest power. Instead, we have been divided, weakened, and at odds over what was meant to give us the key to our salvation. With The Game there is no confusion or division. There's nothing to inflate our egos by reciting stories or using scripture as a sword to cut others down or substantiate our postering. Now we have clear direction, either we honor the rules that are not to be broken or we don't. There will undoubtedly be those who will find The Game to be too demanding, but for those who are diligent, they will reap the reward in unexplainable ways. Much like the Bible that speaks to you personally, The Game will become a part of you, taking on a life of its own. Once you are shown what to look for, you can't unsee it.

Considering all the confusion there is about love, the deception about the truth has affected everyone. The dark cloud discriminates against no one—not the young or old; rich, or poor not the beautiful, unattractive, intelligent, or simple-minded. It doesn't matter if you're a celebrity, a high-powered CEO, or live a humble existence. Hatred, competition, and division live in every sector of our human experience. Pride derived from not knowing our value and self-loathing, we continue to make costly mistakes affecting everyone; it doesn't matter where you are from.

All colors, race, and religion, people from all over the world, suffer from the inability to love themselves and one another correctly in order to reach the Most High dwelling. Although cultures may be different, and some behaviors are more acceptable in places where others are not, what is considered as acceptable behavior often does not equate to love. This book is to help you clearly understand how to recognize, build, and discern impeccable character by learning how to be virtuous to the tune of pure love. In that, your peace and prosperity materialize. With your participation, you can eliminate all of the dire consequences relating to ignorance, allowances, fear, and the misconception of love. For those who would like to spend the rest of their lives experiencing the beauty of God's promise, self-mastery is the way.

The better player you become, the better you will read people's intentions, be able to identify their character, and be steadfast in your own character; which leads to self-worth and confidence. As you practice The Game, you will eliminate the drama in your life, realizing why people do what they do. You will become the watcher. There's no need to take an active role, when you realize it's not your game. Time will become of little concern, as there's no reason to rush; everything is in perfect timing. You'll no longer have a reason to worry because you'll always trust in the goodness of the present. The present is how you take your life back.

With every sun up to sundown, you can look forward to understanding the pieces and the rules, and with proper application, the universe will show you the wonder, amazement, coincidence, and blessing you didn't know how to purposefully access.

The number one rule is to love yourself; that's your relationship with God. Of course, we have a manual, The Bible, but as you can see, it hasn't been very effective because there's more emphasis placed on the opinion of the interpretation rather than on the importance of the execution of the message to love. Often times, the same people who claim to be faithful Christians act contrary to Christ. The Messiah's behavior and his unwavering faith are what set him apart from humanity. The Messiah understood who he was, where he came from, and what he was here to do. The Messiah came into this world, but he's not ruled by the ego. He was born of the Father, a manifestation of love, and not a product of sinful people. He was the example, the embodiment of love, so we could experience God (love) in the flesh.

Love is what we are. But, we have lost our way, becoming an amplified ego—a self-consumed, insecure, faithless being who causes harm to self and others contrary to virtue. Our inability to model the Messiah is the reason for our pain. We are the cause of our own suffering. We consume ourselves with worry instead of living in faith because we lack the confidence that virtuous behavior will keep us protected at the Most High vibration. Religion has not served us well, for many churches have taken our Manual and turned God's Word into a business of fear-based protocols to program the masses instead of teaching the way to love and the real benefits of knowing how to self-govern. Now, we have no excuse for our ignorance. To love is to know God.

Part 6

HOW TO PLAY

The 'how' is simple, but not easy. The game concept helps us to understand how to win at love, but the moves are complex and require a high degree of self-awareness and observation; you must master holding your tongue in order to think before making a move. Mastering The Game requires you to adhere to all the rules, be unconsciously competent with all of the pieces, while keeping the board in the forefront of your mind. If you don't, you'll be subject to handling your affairs the same way you always have.

Now that you're becoming a player, humility is imperative. Regardless of the books you've read, ideology you follow, or religious affiliation, The Game is going to hold you accountable like nothing you've ever experienced. There is no more ambiguity about the right way to behave nor will there be an allowance for "everyone has their own interpretation." The Game is clear. There is no escape once you've been given clarity. At this point, you can stop and choose not to know, live in ignorance, and conduct your life the same as you always have, struggling to get by and get along. It is my hope that you continue on this path so that you too can experience your life as God intended.

The Game is serious business. If not honored, your life story will be worse than before you started because the devil has no mercy. Follow to become supernaturally protected. The more committed you are, the sooner you'll move through your circumstances, changing your ego to love. There's not one situation where your pieces could ever fail you. Knowing this truth, you will look forward to playing each day with the anticipation of changing your failures to success.

Success is something you'll witness according to your move. Favor is an unexpected gift with your name on it. Much like Christmas: there's a tree in the corner filled with gifts large and small with your name on them. There is no competition. As you choose to love, your favored response is delivered. The gifts are unlimited. Some might say, "Oh, I'm not looking for any gifts. I'm fine with what I have." This is an abomination to the Most High. Your life is his delight. There's a plan for you if you would just submit to the instruction. Do what your heart is calling you to do, and everything will be all right. Once you experience the gift once, you will be inspired to experience it again.

There are people, situations, coincidences, and opportunities waiting for you each time you pass the test making love your answer. Passing the test will bring you moments of intense gratitude. I'm not talking about the subdued practice of gratitude; I mean God will take you to your knees, thanking him for what just happened. You will discover his power in the grandest of ways. Put The Game to the test, you'll quickly learn to let go and trust the process.

As soon as you experience a win, you'll know it. The response from people is immediate when you make the right move. If you're not seeing an immediate result from your player, you're not doing it right. It's simple but not easy. Be cautious, open to correction, and patient. These instructions will need time and attention.

Change takes practice. While learning how to play, do not judge others in their ignorance. Instead, show compassion. Acknowledge and Accept without judgment. You have now become a project of great importance. Become the best love, not the best judge.

Every deed, thought, and word will bring a response. The Game is always in play. There's no time out when you're not thinking about it.

The ride is about to begin. Remember, there's no going back, and you can't get out or quit. As long as you're living, The Game is in play. I suggest you keep the concept of the board in your mind and remember, regardless of the situation, amount of people involved, the timeline, or circumstance, there are never more than two players playing at one time.

THE BOARD

Earn your pieces.

The virtues you possess are the pieces you play.

Keep the board in mind until you become at least a moderate player. To lose sight will put your King at risk because you'll forget there are only two players. Remember the concept of the board. A stacked board means you have mastered The Game by filling your board with virtues.

Part 7

THE RULES

These 51 rules represent behaviors contrary to Love; the Ego

No ACCUSATIONS	No DEFENDING	No INTIMIDATING
No PLAYING VICTIM	No "ALWAYS" OR "NEVER"	No DEMANDING
No INTRUDING	No PROMISES	No ASSUMPTIONS
No DEMEANING	No JUDGING	No PUBLIC HUMILIATION
No AVOIDING	No DEVIL'S ADVOCATE	No JUSTIFICATION
No PUBLIC MONEY TALK	No BEGGING	No DISRESPECT
No LAUNDRY LIST	No RATIONALIZING	No BETRAYAL
No DUMPING	No LYING, STEALING, OR CHEATING	
No REDIRECTING	No BLAMING No EXCUSES	No MANIPULATING
No RETALIATION	No BULLDOZING	No EXPECTATIONS
No MIRRORING	No SARCASM	No BULLYING
No GOSSIP	No NAME CALLING	No SCOREKEEPING
No CHALLENGING	No GUILT	No OFFENDING
No SELF-DEPRECATION	No COMPLAINING	No IGNORING
No OVER EXPLAINING	No SELF- PROMOTION	No CONNIVING
No IMPOSING	No PATRONIZING	No THREATENING
No DECEPTION	No INSULTING	No PITY PARTY

Princess Merrilee of Solana

1. No Accusations

This is a common mistake. Do not accuse your player of his intent, thoughts, or actions. Exercise the pause. Make your "move" by asking questions to gain understanding or risk being guilty of making assumptions. Do not ask accusatory questions when the truth is known in hopes of gaining an admission of guilt. Their admission will only bring you to your same move—to move on. You don't need the closure. Instead, make a mental note of the behavior. When your findings are conclusive and their King (honor or integrity) has been lost, it's game over. Now it's time to move away from the table.

When you accuse your player of doing or intending to make a hurtful move, or accuse them according to negative assumptions, you are acting in fear, pushing love away. Your lack of trust in their honor is now evident. This is a very hurtful move that causes the breakdown of the relationship. It is better to ask honest questions, without inferring your suspicions.

2. No "Always" or "Never"

Statements that start with 'always' and 'never' are exaggerated, blanket statements that make you lose credibility with your player and entices them to defend. You don't want to provoke your player to break a rule, ever. Substitute "it's been my experience" or "I haven't noticed that before."

3. No Assumptions

This is the most difficult of rules. It's not easy to recognize when an assumption has been made by you or your player. Ask yourself, how do I know this? Like a traffic light that moves from green to yellow to red, and red to green, don't jump to a conclusion because you already know the direction of the conversation. Wait for evidence of the truth before making a move. Listen and watch carefully to what's being said or done in the present moment before assuming a direction. Avoid interrupting your player's move with a presumption of understanding. To do so will often require an apology. Be careful not to fall victim to the rationale, "I know what he/she is thinking. I know what they meant." You must have clear and present evidence of truth in your understanding to avoid making an assumption. Remain blameless by honoring the rules. Assumptions are a product of future probabilities. There's no need to assume anything in the present moment. If your present moment of understanding is clear without inferring, your next move will be virtuous and honorable.

4. No Avoiding

Avoidance can be an act of fear, or it can be wisdom depending on the reason for it. Fear is having your Queen off the board placing your King in danger. Wisdom is avoiding the rules to stay in favor. Know the difference. Stay in honor, face your challenge.

5. No Begging

To beg is to manipulate. Begging sacrifices self-respect. A loss of self-respect is a loss of honor. There is no honor in begging. Game Over.

6. No Betrayal

Betrayal is seen in many forms of behavior: Any behavior that shows disrespect for your player. Lie, steal, cheat, demean, dishonor, deny, deception, double cross, gossip, or expose. To betray your player is to be anything other than honorable with your relationship. Be truthful, transparent, trustworthy, and clear in your word and deed. False idolatry is betrayal.

7. No Blaming

Careful. Blame and excuses are bed buddies. Be accountable for your part in the game with your player. Accept that you are in control of your move. No person or circumstance has control over your side of the board. Consider where you need to take responsibility for your words, interpretations, and decisions.

8. No Bulldozing

Bulldozing applies when you (or your player) take more than one move that bullies the other into submission. Bulldozing sounds like you can't get a word in edgewise and your player has already made up their mind without your contribution.

9. No Bullying

Never ever resort to bullying anyone for any reason—not a child, spouse, employee, neighbor, or acquaintance. Bullying is a coward's move. There must be no name calling, yelling, threatening, intimidation, humiliation or manipulation of any kind.

10. No Complaining

Don't subject your player to your negativity. Using your player as a sounding board is imposing. Nobody wants to hear their player complaining, never having a solution to the complaint. Acknowledge the issue, find a solution and move on.

11. No Conniving

Any attempt to benefit from your player under the pretense of love, friendship, or relationship in order to have your way will boomerang and hit you straight where it hurts. A broken heart. A broken heart is Game Over.

12. No Challenging

Playing devil's advocate, questioning motives, or acting like you have a right to question your player's business will not gain favor. Do not make a move to put your player on defense. Instead, ask questions to gain clarity from a genuine interest. Any move on your part to cause your player to break the no defending rule is a wrong move. When you challenge your player, you take a position of authority. The only authority you have with your player is to choose to communicate with respect in order to maintain his.

13. No Deception

Do not pretend to be, know, or have more than you are. It doesn't serve you to pad or minimize the truth. The universe is always watching. Untruths come with consequence.

14. No Defending

When accused, do not defend yourself. Instead, ask a question to help your player gain clarity. Keep in mind "how did you arrive at this conclusion?" Work to bring both of you to the same understanding by asking questions instead of defending your position of being right. Pause to consider. Question the accusation by identifying the assumption. Ask 'why' and 'how'..'Avoid 'what' ' 'What' questions tend to be accusatory.

15. No Demanding

You cannot demand that your player show you respect, act with respect, or be any certain way with their behavior. Demanding anything will push your player away from love when you take a position of control. You cannot control your player by demanding anything. Either they will choose to love, or they won't.

16. No Demeaning

Do not cause your player to lose their dignity by insulting their intelligence. Any move to articulate their shortcomings will make you at fault. Let your player be who they are without your verbal assessment. Pause and use your words with diplomacy to remain blameless. Let your player be responsible for their own dignity by allowing their behavior to expose the truth. When in doubt, keep your mouth shut. A mother whose child is acting up in the store is tempted to discipline immediately by threatening, raising her voice, name calling, and sometimes exerting physical force. She's challenged and her ego takes over. When her ego takes over, she is responsible for his pain and diminished self-worth. She is responsible for raising her child in fear instead of love.

When she takes a moment to pause, she is more likely to put the situation in perspective, have self-awareness, and put the child first.

17. NO DEVIL'S ADVOCATE

Be careful when opposing your player's thoughts, plans, pursuits, dreams, decisions, and perspectives. It's not your job to impose the flip side of anything until you are invited to do so. If you make a move that puts doubt or fear in your player, you are getting in the way of their faith; dividing your player from God. The universe does not respond favorably to those who advocate the devil's work. Be sure to check your own fears before imposing them on to others.

18. NO DISRESPECT

Any type of disrespect is unacceptable—an underhanded compliment, insulting your player's intelligence, ignoring their request, dismissing their concerns, denying your ability to help, and breaking any rule on the list. One should always aim to be respectable even when respect is not there.

19. NO DUMPING

Do not dump your third-party drama (gossip, problems, and circumstances and stories) on your player. Dumping is an imposition on your player's time and attention. Do not assume to have their interest. If you feel the need to purge your emotions, it's best to write your feelings on paper and let it go. The paper tells no one. You remain blameless, safe, and in honor. Recognize when your player is guilty of dumping. It's okay to be a friend and listen but use discernment. Know the difference between a pain-body who feeds off their own drama from someone who needs an ear, a hug, someone to understand and a little inspiration. The pain-body suffers from a lack of self-love. No amount of time and attention will save them from their own pain. This is where you exercise self-love and walk away.

20. NO EXCUSES

Excuses are similar to rationalizing, as both imply blame without accountability. Don't make excuses for your actions or decisions. Take the time to think about your move so you don't have to make excuses. Should you break a rule, accept responsibility, correct if you can and move on. It's very easy to make excuses for external events and circumstances that appear to be out of our control. Excuses are not necessary. Stick to what is without overexplaining. Your player will very rarely care about why; they only care about what is. Be very cautious to recognize when a rule has been broken, because one broken rule can easily lead to another broken rule. It's a slippery slope that happens very fast. Slow down. It won't be easy, but your character is worth it.

21. NO EXPECTATIONS

This is one of the hardest rules to follow. Don't expect your player to respond the way you think they should. Don't expect your player to know what you want. Don't expect your player to understand without further clarification. Don't expect your player to give you a turn or respect your boundaries. Watch yourself carefully. Drop all expectations. Learn to watch and accept the move. You don't know your player's next move; do not try to anticipate, predict, or act before the move is made. Be still and wait for your truth to come to pass.

22. NO GOSSIPING

Gossip is spreading information that doesn't concern you or your player. There are only two players. To talk about your player with others who are not in play is gossiping. Never bring others into play with your player in order to substantiate your claim, prove blame, make a point, secure your argument, or to expose irrelevant information about the business of others that are not involved in your present moment.

23. No Guilt

Guilt serves no one. Never try to manipulate your player by imposing guilt upon them for any reason. Never allow someone else to use guilt as a tool to manipulate you. Be careful to recognize this move. "I'm never right," or, "Oh, I guess it's my fault again," or, "You're never wrong, are you?" Or, "It's okay, you don't have to do it." Or, "Well, if you hadn't, I wouldn't have…" Blame and guilt go hand in hand. If your player is trying to guilt you into doing something, you can bet their manipulation won't stop there.

24. No Ignoring

To ignore your player is disrespectful. Return the text, call, or give the attention needed in the moment. At the very least, acknowledge the move. Ask a question, can you hold on, give me a moment or can I call you back? Protect your King first by being respectful. When someone other than your player is disrespectful, or dishonorable, ignore it if it's not your game unless, of course, someone is in physical danger.

25. No Imposing

Visualize moving beyond your side of the board to play the other side for your player. Back up. Maintain your boundary by staying on your side. Do not impose your will, desire, opinion, expectation, direction, knowledge, presence, time, needs, or favors onto your player. Never think you are within your right to act against another, make decisions for, express your contempt, or expect your player to conform to your wishes. Demonstrate self-respect by asking for permission before assuming you can impose. One example is time: Do not disrespect your player's time by filling it with information of little interest. It's better to attract your player's interest and inquiry, than to assume it. Storytelling is fine when your story is relevant to them, but don't assume your player has an unlimited attention span by imposing stories with no conclusion. Never take more time than your player is willing to give.

26. NO INSULTING

Accusations and assumptions lead to insults. Insults are a blatant disrespect for your player. Do not be tempted to defend yourself against an insult. Better to recognize the move knowing the rule has been broken. When you are insulted by your player, lead with a question. Are you saying that I am... or, say I don't understand. This gives your player an opportunity to rephrase what has been said. Sometimes we would like to take back what we've said, so it's good to give that opportunity to your player. Insults are often a lack of grace or diplomacy.

27. NO INTIMIDATING

Never purposely use your position, status, knowledge, confidence, looks, money, degrees, or accolades to make your player feel inferior to you. This is an ego-based move, not love.

28. NO INTRUDING

Remember, The Game never has more than two players. Do not intrude on someone else's game. As a spectator to others, don't interfere with their moves. Even when invited to join, remember that The Game switches between you and the one that invited you—not you and the original two players. If you're asked to take sides in an argument, be objective and ask questions that will help the others gain clarity. Don't take a side, aim to expose the truth.

29. NO JUDGING

Judgment is to make a premature assessment without taking the time to learn enough to have an accurate, unbiased opinion. Oftentimes judgment is an assessment based on insecurities or ignorance. Practice asking questions to gain a clear understanding.

30. NO JUSTIFICATION

Justification is rationalizing poor behavior when a rule has been broken. Don't do it. If you are guilty of breaking a rule, it's best to own it. Act with honor. Be careful to consider before justifying your move with excuses, blame, and accusations. If you are without a virtuous move, Acknowledge and Accept. It is best to hold your tongue and take no action rather than break a rule to try and cover for your mistake.

31. NO LAUNDRY LIST

Never remind your player of all the wrong moves they've made or all of the right moves you think you've made. This will cause resentment in your player and you'll lose their trust. Best to be aware of their moves and know when to call Game Over after they've lost your trust. When you are discussing a problem, don't have any expectations for your player's behavior. How they behave is their decision. Be the watcher and recognize when you've lost respect. It's now Game Over.

32. NO LYING, STEALING, CHEATING

These rules should be obvious and need no explanation. However, due to the small infractions that are easily dismissed, I added these for those who don't realize it's not okay to tell little white lies, help yourself without asking, or fudge a little when no one is looking. Get caught once, and it's Game Over.

33. NO MANIPULATING

Never make a move with ulterior motives or with anticipation of your player's next move. Manipulation happens when you try to predict the probable outcome when contemplating your player's thoughts and responses. These premeditated moves will bring you more trouble because they are methods of control rather than real-time virtuous responses. You will ultimately lose respect from your player and maybe the respect of spectators if they see you manipulate a situation. If you can't get what you want honorably, don't do it. Any coercing, bribing, bullying or threatening behavior will result in unforeseen problems without a foreseeable end.

34. No Mirroring

Do not avoid confrontation by mirroring your player's move. The question,'Where were you last night? The mirror. Where were you last weekend? The question. How much money did you spend? The mirror. How much money do you spend every day?' Just answer the question without taking offense. Contrary to popular belief, do not answer a question with a question. It will signal to your player that you are on the defense. When questioned, provide a clear and direct answer with one move. Wait for your player's move before proceeding.

35. No Name Calling

Never use derogatory names toward anyone at any time. This includes all foul language, profanity, cursing and playfully negative pet names. You will lose your honor in an instant anytime you hurt your player. You will lose your player's trust. Where trust is absent, the game cannot continue. Even when you think it's okay to have a derogatory pet name, you'll lose their respect for your character. Don't do it.

36. No Offending

Have self-awareness. Do not use offensive language, disrespectful references, insult your player's knowledge of something, or impose distasteful personal habits onto your player. Nobody appreciates belches, passing gas, embarrassing behavior, or a blatant disrespect for another's intelligence, their perspective on life, or their standard of living.

37. No Overexplaining

You have one move. Say what you have to say with simplicity and clarity. If your player doesn't understand, they will ask for further clarification. Do not assume they don't understand by continuing to overexplain yourself, giving multiple stories, and analogies to correct your previous statement.

38. No Patronizing

Patronizing is to talk down to your player, presuming you know more or better. It's an insult to your player's intelligence. It's a sign for your player to recognize that you don't respect them.

39. No Pity Party

No one respects a player who feels sorry for themselves. Avoid complaining about your skills or shortcomings to your player—acknowledge them and work to improve. Your skills are between you and your Maker. If you need help, ask your player with sincerity. Don't hint around or guilt them into offering.

40. No Playing Victim

A victim takes a position of innocence, holding no responsibility for their part in the exchange. A victim mentality is a powerless and weak position of claiming not to have a choice, which is never respected. Honorable behavior is to Acknowledge and Accept what has happened without blaming your response move on your player. You always have a choice to leave with self-respect and be respectful toward your player.

41. No Promises

When you realize you've made a mistake, apologize. Do not insert a future promise, "I'll make it up to you next time." This will only set you up for expectations and failure when you forget, which leads to a loss of trust (integrity). Make a move without making a promise or announcement. Should you make a promise, keep it in a timely fashion, or you'll lose your King without realizing it.

42. No Public Humiliation

Never call out your player in public. Whether it's your significant other, your child, or the lady at the DMV, never humiliate yourself or others by making a spectacle of yourself, no matter how angry you are. Remember the pause. Maintain your dignity, hold your tongue, walk away if you don't know the right thing to say. Think about your King first. Mastery requires self-discipline.

43. No Public Money Talk

Don't embarrass your player by discussing finances in mixed company. Don't assume that you have a right to your player's business. They will not appreciate the imposition of the exposure. Don't impose your questions with the expectation that your player will oblige with an answer. Always handle money and finances in private.

44. No Rationalizing

Do not rationalize poor behavior, neither your own or your player's. When the right move is made, there is no need for explanation. Only a wrong move will cause you to explain yourself. Take the time to think before making a move to avoid rationalizing. A virtuous move never needs explaining.

45. No Redirecting

When your player makes a move, don't divert their attention toward irrelevant distractions to avoid their move.

Player A: "Why didn't you make the deposit today?"

Player B: "Do you know how many things I have to do in a day?"

Player A: "So you were too busy?"

Player B: "Nothing went right today, I almost ran out of gas, then I almost hit a dog. Can I just have some peace and quiet please?"

Notice, the player made one move to the other's four moves. There was a question by player A, followed by a challenge, insult, complaint, and redirect by player B. Player B has lost his integrity as he avoided the question. Player A has cause not to trust. The King has left the board. It's Game Over. They may continue to push the pieces around, but the trust is lost.

46. No Retaliation

Retaliation is the inability to forgive. To retaliate shows a lack of emotional maturity. If you feel the need to retaliate, it's Game Over.

47. No Sarcasm

It takes a sharp wit to use sarcasm without offending. Unlike humor, sarcasm is hurtful. It's also exhausting, as it's difficult for your player to continue giving a courtesy laugh. Sarcasm originates from pain. It's a surefire way to show your insecurities.

48. No Scorekeeping

Never play the 'my turn, your turn,' or 'I did this, so you do that," game. 'I fed the dogs last time, it's your turn.' 'Why do I always have to do the dishes? You never do them.' Be honorable, just take care of business. If a clear imbalance presents itself, pay close attention to other ways you may be making allowances for your player's behavior.

49. No Self-Deprecation

To overuse humor to make fun of yourself makes your player feel sorry for you. If your player feels sorry for you, they won't respect you.

50. No Self-Promotion

Marketing is not the same as self-promotion. Marketing is what is said on paper, online, and in the media. When in-person, do not tell your player who or what you think you are and all your accomplishments—statements like, "I'm funny, good looking, intelligent, fit, attractive, handy, number one, an awesome cook," or other accomplishments or personal attributes. Your player may not care or agree. If you self-proclaim what you are, you may discourage your player from expressing their genuine impression of you. Be humble. Let others do the talking for you. Do not share with your player what others have said about you to support your ego. Allow your player to get to know your attributes, naturally discovering who you are as The Game progresses. Premature disclosure will make you appear self-absorbed, boastful, and egotistical. None which are respectable attributes. This behavior will cause your player to disengage and not trust you.

51. No Threatening

Never threaten to quit, leave, hurt, or commit to something in hopes of hurting or controlling your player. A threat is dishonorable behavior. Game Over.

Although this list is extensive, it's not exhaustive. Simply said, be kind. If your behavior does not feel good, honorable, and admirable, it probably isn't. The universe's response will be your guide. Life will respond. Rest assured, you will experience favor or consequence. Either way, it's coming. There is no escape. All actions, thoughts, and plans will be brought to light. If you pay attention, you'll see how favor is slotted for the virtuous.

Part 8

THE PIECES

"Moral virtues are the attitudes, dispositions, and good habits that govern one's actions, passions, and conduct according to reason and are acquired by human effort."

~Immanuel Kant

The pieces represent your virtues. Virtues are not given. They must be earned in order to be placed on the board. The more pieces you're able to master, the more solid your character. Each acquired piece helps to protect your Honor and Integrity. Your King remains firmly on the board each time you move without breaking a rule. Until you master your virtues, your King is at risk with every move, with every player. Without virtue, your behavior, by default, reverts to breaking the rules.

Virtues are acquired by an awareness of concentrated effort.
Without focused attention and development, none will exist.

List of 23 Virtues

HONOR & INTEGRITY

FAITH

PATIENCE

LOYALTY

TOLERANCE

ACKNOWLEDGE & ACCEPT

FORGIVENESS

MERCY

DIPLOMACY

HUMILITY

COMPASSION

HUMOR

CHARITY

WISDOM

DISCERNMENT

NOBILITY

RESPECT, RESPECTFUL, RESPECTABLE

GRACE

RESILIENCE

CONTRIBUTION

GRATITUDE

EDIFICATION

TEMPERANCE

KING

Honor and Integrity

The King represents your *Honor and Integrity*. To be honorable is to maintain a noble disposition of self-respect by exhibiting respectful behavior toward your player regardless of whether you respect them or they are respectable. *Honor* is to possess a high moral standard for self, being trustworthy, and demonstrating an unshakable moral compass. To be honorable is to refrain from all dishonorable behavior.

Integrity is the value of your word; do as you say and take pride in what you do. Use extreme caution before making a move as the King can be lost in as little as one move—not just the next move, but the first move in play. One wrong first move could be Game Over. When in doubt, keep your mouth shut. When the King is lost, it cannot be regained by you or your player. You must acknowledge the move, accept the disappointment of the loss, and walk away from the board. No explanations, defenses, allowances, exceptions, or denial. Honor thyself first (God). To continue playing the game without Honor or Integrity is to unnecessarily prolong a more painful inevitable end. As soon as trust is lost, the relationship is over. Do not sacrifice your integrity by continuing to play when your player's King is missing from the board.

You might be wondering if you can forgive, start over, and allow the relationship to continue. You can, but to make allowances is foolish. A relationship without trust is over. It's time to walk away. In years to come, your player may come back to the board after time lends opportunity for growth and a change in behavior. But never assume an apology will create an immediate change in your player. There's no incentive to change once the apology is accepted. However, be extremely cautious before calling Game Over. Be sure to check yourself to see if you've made an assumption or if you've been offended by an unfulfilled expectation. That's on you. You must have evidence of your player's dishonorable behavior before you call Game Over. Otherwise, your miscalculation will result in the loss of your King as your emotional response triggers a list of rules broken. Do not rely on hearsay and third-party rumors. The move must be directly played on the board with you in real time. Should you witness your player's dishonorable behavior with another player, be cautious in your own game by becoming the watcher. As the watcher, you become highly aware of your player's moves, anticipating the move to cause Game Over. When you witness dishonorable behavior with another, know it will happen to you.

Remember that all of your thoughts, actions and behaviors are known by the universe. Your honor will depend on how you show respectful behavior toward others, how you demonstrate respectable behavior for yourself, and your virtuous disposition that earns you respect from each player. Your integrity is your unimpaired promise to respect your word and deed. Each time you make an allowance for yourself, others are watching. When you think an allowance is okay for yourself, others may not be so forgiving. Keep your King on the board or you may end up alone.

QUEEN

Faith

The Queen represents your Faith. Your Queen is the most powerful and most important piece on the board. Her presence enables you to slow down to make wise and knowledgeable decisions regarding your perspective, perception, framing, and the best action to take with your virtues. To have faith is to let go of trying to control people, circumstances, and their level of awareness by acknowledging and accepting what is right now with patience. You are not to play your player's game. Do not lose faith in their ability to make the right move or their ability to survive the consequence resulting from a wrong move. Do not try to warn them of wrong moves in an attempt to save yourself from having to make a tough decision. Honor the boundary by staying on your side of the board.

To have faith is to believe in something greater than yourself that is within yourself. This is the universe watching, aiding, testing, rewarding, and recording all of your thoughts, actions, intentions, and decisions. You are always in play with yourself, so it's best to take a position that the universe is always working in your favor to help you in perfect timing. When your faith is not on the board, you will make regretful decisions (moves) based on fearful thinking.

Watch yourself closely as your emotions will be the first to let you know that your Queen is off the board. Decisions made in fear feel like doubt, anxiety, loss, confusion, overthinking, loneliness, stress, anger, restlessness, impatience, depression, and an overall feeling of being out of control. These emotions will lead to breaking the rules which will result in a loss of your King.

Consider and reconsider your need for control over your player and your circumstances along with the emotions that prevent you from letting go of the need for that perception of control. The stronger your need for control, the more your ego is in charge and the more often your Queen is off the board. It's highly unlikely you'll be able to execute a timely Virtue. For example, you are wrongly accused. You are angry. Your first response is to defend yourself instead of moving a Virtue. Use Patience to ask a non-accusatory question then pause for their move. Without having Faith in your ability to pause, you will struggle to maintain respect from your player.

Should you lose your King, know that it was the devil (your ego), that was put before your faith in God. The ego will try to control your circumstances, but faith will control your behavior by responding in Virtue. Remember that the Queen (Faith) can be lost for a moment, but also regained in an instant when you are aware that she's off the board. Heighten your awareness to know when she's off the board. She will be your guide when you are in doubt about your next move. Be still and listen. Your answer will be delivered. Know that it will. To have faith is to pause before responding to your fears and wait for the universe to provide the answer without you making premature decisions in fear. If there is no clear and present danger, use patience to help you get your queen on the board.

Be careful to keep in mind, the moment you're in play without your Queen on the board, you are more likely to behave with non-loving behavior than you are to respond with virtue. Aim to maintain your Honor and Integrity, be faithful, and keep your ego in check. It's less important to be heard or understood. You don't have to be right. You don't have to defend your position. Wait for the opportunity to make the right move with your Virtue. Faith is waiting in silence to take a pause to allow the universe to guide you to your next move. To keep your Queen on the board means to believe that the universe is your partner. You need not take an offensive position in life. Wait, listen, and ask questions sincerely.

Having faith means you are able to take your time to make the right move again, even when you see the game coming to an end because your trust in your player is beginning to wane. The importance of Faith is to slow down to allow both your player and the universe to guide your next move. Do not jump to conclusions. Allow your player to move. The universe can redirect your move with new information and circumstances. So, it's important to allow rather than control. Small incremental moves allow faith to take over as you let go of expectations, fear, and assumptions.

When you make one move at a time you receive more information each time your player moves, which gives you greater understanding. Faith says I'm not in a hurry. For example, you're on the edge of a breakup. You get an annoying text that feels like the last straw. What you want to do is end the relationship. You can't. The game does not end over an annoyance. It must be the result of a loss of Trust. Pay close attention to the exact moment the Trust is lost. Until then, keep your responses respectful with each move being virtuous. To have Faith is to know that you will recognize the final move when it happens. There's no reason to anticipate with fear of it happening. The longer you're able to respond with love, the longer you'll stay in play. Your behavior with each move is more important than the enormity of any situation. Because every situation is a test to see if you will break a rule or respond with love. Faith keeps you on the straight and narrow. If you realize that you don't trust your player, but you're still in play, it means you missed Game Over. It's okay. Stay respectful and respectable. Stop investing and move away from the table.

Faith protects your King. Faith is prayer. Faith is meditation. Faith is strength in humility. Faith allows us to be still when we're anxious. Faith shows us how to be patient. Faith pushes us to love harder when we're insecure. Faith allows us to let go when our ego is screaming to control. Faith says your answer is coming; you don't need to know right now. Faith is believing you have angels to protect you and guides to lead you. Faith is knowing you don't have to be perfect when your behavior aligns with virtue. Faith is knowing that you hold the key to the universe inside of you. You are the greatest power, the love of your life, and the answer to your prayer. Faith is knowing that all of your favor is created one move at a time.

"If you love me, you will obey what I command and I will ask
the Father and he will give you another counselor
to be with you forever the Spirit of truth"

John 14:15-17

If you love "me" you will obey the command to love.
If I believe that I have Christ/God in me, then loving myself is
the same as loving God. The Spirit of Truth is your intuition,
the counselor and guide is love. Listen to your heart and be
disciplined in the ways of love to keep you blameless.

A complete board means you've mastered your virtues.

Take inventory of your Virtues. If you have less than the Virtues listed, it's okay; you're not alone. You now have a list of what you need to work toward. Just be cautious as you're learning because you don't have pieces on the board to protect your King yet. There's no time out for a learning curve. You're in play right now with or without your Virtues. Get familiar with each piece, learn what they mean, and how to play them. I suggest you start with Patience. Patience will help you keep your Queen on the board to protect your King. Without Patience, the frustration of your learning curve might discourage your commitment and your progress as you lose faith in the gift of the game.

It's not easy to hold yourself accountable to such a high level of play. But your diligence will serve you well the longer you stay committed. The longer you stay committed, the more committed you become. Self-mastery places you among the elite players who know the complexity of love by using multiple pieces in one move. With each piece you master, your confidence will grow and your commitment to love will elevate your standard of self-love. Each virtuous decision helps you through the toughest circumstances with ease. Your priority is to maintain your King—your Honor and Integrity. Protect yourself at all times and do not fall into the trap of reacting in a like-for-like move. You'll find that most people play contrary to Love and break all the rules.

Now that you've been introduced to The Game, you're responsible. Focus on the complexity of each piece as there are many facets in their application. Self-mastery is achieved with focus attention to each virtue. With each piece you add to the board you become empowered and able to recognize the missing pieces on your player's side of the board. With your attention, the fate of your relationships with the people you've played with in the past becomes noticeably clear as their behavior, or maybe yours, broke the rules and lost a King.

1. Honor and Integrity

The simplest way to remain in honor is to keep your mouth shut and your head held high, especially when your character is under attack or when the character of your player is in question. Do not be tempted to defend yourself, instead seek to understand your accuser. The best defense is to ask a pure and honest question to gain clarity on their perspective about you or the circumstance. Recognize the assumption, accusation, or other rules broken while under attack. Protect your King by maintaining self-respect. Do not yell, accuse, defend, deny, make excuses, avoid or over explain your position. Acknowledge and accept their move by apologizing for the infraction (your one move) and allow them to make their next move. Do not infringe on their move. Be respectful to listen and observe without interruption.

When your player is hurt, they will make moves to hurt you. Be the watcher, keep the rules in mind, and don't take offense. Do not mirror their move (answer a question with the same question). Recognize your opportunity to execute a virtue. Have patience, use grace (say the right thing at the right time). You get one move. Stop and let them make their move before taking another. To stay in honor, you must be respectful of your player—never mind the circumstance or perspective that fueled their move. To protect your King, you must be respectable. Be sure that your behavior is blameless.

Keep your ego and emotions in check by exercising the pause. Consider your players move before making a move. The moment you or your player break a rule, *respect* is lost. To lose respect means the King is in jeopardy. Be respectful of each player, one player at a time. If your child disrespects you, pause and proceed with caution. The example you set takes precedence before being right about the circumstance. To stay in honor, you must honor your child by being respectful. Do not bully, overpower or try to control him with threats, yelling, or demean with name calling. Your King is at stake, especially with your child. You can't demand respect; you must maintain it. The example you set today will determine your relationship tomorrow. Teach your child to respect you from a place of love and adoration not from a place of fear and control.

The same is true for every player no matter the relationship, gender, age, or background. Honor is maintained when your behavior is the example of love.

Integrity is a unified mind, body, and spirit. People presume to have integrity but fail to recognize the behaviors that prove them to be divided. To be unified is to align the ego-mind with the moral compass of the heart to model honorable behavior. The ego makes allowances for poor behavior, integrity refutes it. The common definition for integrity is to be impeccable with your word. However, it's not enough to keep your word, or to say what you mean and mean what you say. To have integrity is to keep your promise to yourself. Know what is not necessary to say and refrain from saying it. If you add a zinger to the end of your statement, thought, or opinion, you will hurt your player. That unnecessary power play causes your player to lose trust and respect. It's your job to be discerning about the words you choose to say. It won't be easy to refrain from an underhanded or purposeful threat, warning, or snide remark. The consequence to saying more than what is necessary is that you reveal that you don't have a boundary which makes you dangerous. Be mindful of your words. The pause will give you time to consider what you're about to say before you say it without a filter.

2. FAITH

Faith believes in miracles. Faith knows there are angels that guide and protect you from evil. Faith knows you have access to a greater force within you and around you as the universe is always working in your favor. Faith believes in the power of sound frequency, music, vibration, singing bowls, tuning forks, grounding, sun gazing, meditation, and breath work. Faith knows the natural healing modalities of love, laughter, crying, vision, prophecy. Faith believes in natural healing, intention, Reiki, acupuncture, detox, water therapy, and walking in nature. Faith provides a wholesome, true answer for every adversity. God is love. Love is everything true. God endows many gifts to help you along the path home. If you find yourself worrying about things you can't control, remember the goodness that's working in your favor and put those things to work.

3. PATIENCE

Patience is the ability to wait without contempt, anxiety, or need for control. It's the power of the pause. The power of the pause is invaluable because the more you master the pause, the more trust you'll have in your Queen. Patience requires faith and faith requires patience. It's difficult to have one without the other because without faith, you won't know what you're waiting for, and without patience, you won't experience what faith can deliver.

These two pieces are imperative to your success. Watch carefully to determine whether you are waiting for direction from your Queen, and when your player is waiting for you to move. Are you using a virtue or breaking the no ignoring and no avoiding rule? There's a nuance between waiting for direction and being disrespectful toward your player. When you are struggling with the right words to say, at least acknowledge your players move by saying "can you give me a minute? I want to give this my full attention." This tells your player you are respectful and present. Do not defer the move you are able to make in the present. Acknowledgment is all you need to make the next move your player's. Should he have the patience to wait until you resume your attention, your move is to maintain your integrity by picking up where you left off.

The pause becomes invaluable as you discover how to illuminate your player's lack of patience. A lack of patience will further prove the lack of character. The pause is your opportunity to observe information and circumstances to gain the correct perspective about your move and your player. Use caution not to impose on your player's game when you think his move will affect your own. Patience requires temperance; restraint. When you use restraint, you discover how to use the nuances of your virtues. When you learn the nuance of patience, moving one step at a time, you stay on the straight and narrow to receive your blessing.

Practice responding to the world around you with purposeful consideration of your virtues instead of acting with reactive behaviors of control.

4. LOYALTY

Loyalty can be confusing when circumstances become complex, especially when you have information about many different players. Who can you trust, what can you share and what move will put your King at risk? Your first priority is loyalty to your highest self. This is your relationship with God. Stay true to love with every move. Do not sacrifice your relationship with God in the interest of serving others. To love God first is to keep your behavior in alignment with honor and integrity no matter how difficult the move. When you are accused, do not defend. When you are disrespected, do not correct. Know the difference between self-sacrifice and consideration. Know the difference between assumption and confirmation. Loyalty is to know the difference between the rules and the pieces, then choosing to love yourself first through self-discipline.

5. TOLERANCE

Tolerance is the combination of patience and detachment. When you are able to objectively watch your player and know when you are a spectator of other games, you don't take moves personally. When you don't take moves personally, you can recognize which *gate* your player is playing in. Tolerance will invoke compassion as you grow to understand your player's level of play. Your player may not meet your standard of behavior, be tolerant knowing he's just not there yet.

6. ACKNOWLEDGE AND ACCEPT

Acknowledgment recognizes the move without judgment and accept receives the truth without defending. Ask questions to gain clarity. "How and why" questions are receptive to your player. "I hear you; how did I make you feel this way?" When you ask "what" questions, your player is more inclined to defend or accuse. "what did I do wrong or what did I say?" These are defensive responses. When you ask, "how could I have said that better?" you are humble in your invitation for correction. Aim to use your virtues with every move.

7. FORGIVENESS

Forgiveness is non-existent when you reach Spiritual Enlightenment. To be Spiritually Enlightened means there is 'no victim' and 'no blame.' Acknowledge your player's move and accept what you cannot change. Any injustice imposed by your player is contrary to his favor. Do not judge, be offended, keep account, or seek revenge. Instead, show compassion. The moment his debt is created, payment is required. Have faith, the universe always collects. It's not your job to keep account.

You and your player are responsible to the Most High; this is your vertical relationship with God, not your horizontal relationship with each other. With each move you make, be confident not to regret it. Each time you make a move in haste, forgiveness becomes the crutch. We have been taught to expect forgiveness because we have been taught not to hold a grudge. We have been indoctrinated to sacrifice our self-respect in the name of loving our brother. We have been indoctrinated to tolerate dishonor by lowering the standard. Each time we enable our player's lack of character, we become a proponent of the same behavior. Do not expect your player to forgive your move. To ask for forgiveness means your King has been lost but you expect trust to be restored to continue the relationship. It's too late when the trust is gone, there's nothing to forgive. Like a shattered window, the relationship will never be the same. The remainder of your time together will be an attempt to hold it together.

Forgiveness is a construct for the ego's lower realm of understanding. At first, we learn to expect and extent forgiveness. Then we rise to the understanding that forgiveness is meant for our own healing. It's to our benefit to let go of the painful emotional weight we carry. Finally, we elevate to an enlightened understanding; where love resides, forgiveness becomes obsolete. Forgiveness is non-existent when virtuous behavior causes no pain.

8. MERCY

Mercy is an act of restraint. It is to hold back from executing a response that is considered a rational consequence toward your player. When your player has acted dishonorably or without integrity, show mercy by minding your responses. Never gossip, betray, accuse, or defame your player's name in retaliation. Let go and let God. Nothing is worth the price of losing your place of favor.

9. DIPLOMACY

Diplomacy is the order of words in a sentence and the choice of words used to communicate. Your response should include acknowledging and accepting your player's truth without defending your position. Do not provide information without relevance or use emotional or foul language to emphasize your position. Diplomacy is the ability to relate your position without offending your player in order to encourage conversation. When you can effectively choose your words, you will master the rule of no offending.

10. HUMILITY

*Humility is an expression of gratitude so deep that you are
inspired to dedicate your whole life to God in a feeble attempt
to reciprocate the blessing.*

~Princess Merrilee of Solana

To be humble is to be modest about who you think you are, what you know, and any superiority you may believe you have. Humility is authentic and transparent submission with respect to the Spirit in you and your player. Humility happens when you realize you haven't succeeded at using *only your virtues* to communicate, thus being the cause of your pain. To identify humility in your player, listen carefully for respectful language, patience, and questions to facilitate understanding. Observe who he thinks he is, what he knows, and the superiority he believes he's earned. Arrogance screams while humility whispers. It's not necessary for you to inform. To be humble is to listen with the intention to understand your player without needing to "trump" him with your arrogance.

11. COMPASSION

Compassion is showing empathy toward your player. To have compassion is to recognize what is without judging the cause of what is. Have compassion for those who do not yet know The Game. Without having self-awareness or an understanding of love, there will be many people who will disappoint you. Show compassion with patience.

12. HUMOR

Know when and how to say something humorous without ridicule, insult, shame, or sarcasm. Humor is the ability to make something funny without hurting anyone. The moment you injure your players self-worth, you lose trust and respect; your King.

13. Charity

Charity is to give without the expectation of a return. Practice a giving heart. Regardless of circumstance, when you are able to give, do it. Whether its money, a compliment, a smile, or a helping hand, do not postpone until tomorrow what you can give today. Remember, God has given you all that you need to give all that you have... today. Each time you give unto others, more will be given unto you.

14. Wisdom

Wisdom is Truth. The only truth is love. If it's not love, it's not true. The Messiah is the manifestation of love. His example is the truth and the way to attaining wisdom. When we follow his example of love with all of our relationships and encounters with people and circumstances, we gain wisdom. Observe your player and the circumstances. Knowledge is to know the difference between the rules and the pieces. Wisdom is knowing how and when to use them.

15. Discernment

Discernment begins with recognizing whose game is in play. As you begin to see the distinction, you'll be able to recognize the Five Gates which will further help you to identify your players. Discernment gives you the ability to respond to the correct player at the correct time with the correct virtue.

16. Nobility

Those who are noble demonstrate a strong ethical and moral compass knowing the power of self-discipline. They are impervious to pressure and bribery, incorruptible, unselfish, and heroic. They will stand for the powerless, lead with valor, and take a back seat to let others shine.

17. Respectful, Respectable, Respect

Each of these virtues is not like the other. As a master player, you want to conduct your behavior in a *respectful* manner to demonstrate love toward your brother. Self-awareness will help you be *respectable* in the eyes of your brother. If you want *respect*, you will need to earn it. Be careful not to presume to have your player's respect when they are respectful toward you and behave respectably. Respect comes when your player is witness to your self-mastery; honor, integrity, respectful and respectable along with the other virtues. Although your player may not articulate what they've witnessed, their behavior will confirm their respect for you. When you've earned your player's respect, they will edify you, submit to your authority, protect your reputation, and remain loyal in their commitment to you. Until then, your player is only being respectful and respectable. Your player may not disrespect you but will show no sign of respect.

18. GRACE

Grace is knowing what to say and when to say it. It's about the way you communicate. Much like diplomacy but with the addition of timing. To have grace is to demonstrate self-restraint. Maintain self-respect by being respectful even when your player is disrespectful toward you. Your player's lack of self-respect gives evidence of no boundary. When there's no boundary there is no King. When you are challenged, express only what is necessary; nothing more. Do not embellish, add drama, reason or rationale. Grace is to express yourself respectfully and concisely to your player in one move. Grace is also the ability to remain quiet until the opportunity to express a virtue presents itself. To add grace to your board, you must refrain from self-serving, reckless, and impetuous communication. Grace is often the last virtue mastered.

19. RESILIENCE

Resilience is the ability to stay the course in spite of negative circumstances or challenges that may cloud your judgment or hinder your path to love. Resilience is to see the silver lining and keep moving through your adversity with a cheerful heart knowing the universe is working in your favor as long as you're on top of your game.

20. CONTRIBUTION

Contribution is a proactive effort to show your involvement. Give a helping hand, practice active listening, express your ideas, verbalize your thoughts, offer a solution, and give monetary gifts. It's important to elevate your awareness of your player, the situation, and the surrounding circumstances to know what is proper to contribute and when. Your presence is visible. Your contribution or lack of it will be noticed. Keep in mind that people need your contribution even when your self-worth is suffering. Practice contribution and your value becomes apparent.

21. GRATITUDE

Gratitude is to express appreciation for the gift of life and all its wonder. In its simplest form, gratitude is to reciprocate good emotional, psychological, and physiological vibration back to the universe. You can navigate your life experience through gratitude. When you focus on love, being grateful for God's favor in all things, you will be given more reason to be grateful. Each time you acknowledge the silver lining of goodness in your circumstances, your mind, body, and soul resonate with everything you desire, bringing it closer to you. It's that simple. Your life continues to get more magical!

22. EDIFICATION

Edification is the ability to verbally acknowledge beauty and character in everything and everyone around you. Edification is difficult when you have insecurities about yourself, especially when you view the world and your player as a competitor. Change your mindset from competition to appreciation. Practice seeing the beauty in the world around. This will help you to clear your heart and throat chakra to improve your virtuous communication. When you speak love into the world, gratitude fills your heart. The bigger your heart, the more adorable you become.

23. TEMPERANCE

Temperance is the gift of restraint. Control the length of your pause to master emotional responses. Practice seeing through the eyes of moderation to determine the urgency of your move. Find the balance between acknowledging your player's move and making your own. Patience says you have time to consider. Temperance is to care about your player's move, but not so much that you risk losing your King by acting out of turn with emotional responses. Aim to control your thinking, perspective, and response before controlling your player. Moderation is the balance that sees both sides, while patience waits for circumstances to find their center. Don't let people or circumstances break your character. During stressful situations control your temper. Every adversity is an opportunity to build your character and prove yourself to be love.

Part 9

KNOWLEDGE OF THE GAME

With the correct understanding, knowledge of The Game will establish your standard of behavior. When you realize that you are responsible for your moves and no one else's, you understand the boundary. Stay on your side of the board no matter what you see or recognize on the other side. You are not responsible for your player's moves. Be careful not to let your ego and need for control warn your player about their move. Stay on your side. You don't want to impose and interfere with your player exposing their character. Wait and watch their move quietly to assess their understanding of love. If they fall short, losing their King, you must have the courage to walk away as required to love yourself first. Be accountable to love; self-love. Think of yourself as the guardian at the gate. You are not to prioritize anyone before God. Stay high in the tower of virtue. Never lower your standard of behavior to meet your player at their level. Wait for your player to rise.

The Game requires a sharp sense of awareness as the complexity of consciousness moves from a three-dimensional board, rules, and pieces, to the fourth dimension of time recognized as faith, and finally the fifth dimension of self-realization, being conscious of pure love. The sum of these parts can be graphed with The Five Gates. The goal being Spiritually Enlightened. In the beginning, it is common to be lost without a move as you avoid breaking the rules. Be still and wait. The universe will guide you.

Adding pieces to the board requires a conscious awareness of the piece that is missing and a multifaceted understanding of how the virtue is applicable to know when and how to use that piece. To presume to know without observation is the same as not knowing. You'll miss your queue. Those who fail to focus on their pieces will miss most every test with every move with every player. Every potential blessing, opportunity, and relationship will be subject to unfortunate consequence when Virtues are not in play. Virtuous behavior will determine the favor that follows you. Faith is vital to your success. Without faith in the omnipotent, the ego of man—a product of the material world—will never reach the ideal of Spiritual Enlightenment. Keep your Queen on the board and check yourself. She will help you be patient with matters outside of your control, she will help you be tolerant of your player's ignorant behavior, and she will give you answers to help you with your direction. Without Faith, fear will run rampant in your mind and cause a downward spiral of very poor behavior. Poor behavior is aligned with negative thinking. There is no limit to the destruction caused by negative thinking and there is no limit to what Faith can provide. Stay present moment-to-moment. Slow down. Consider the importance of your One Move.

Each time you master a Virtue, the act of self-love empowers you to master another Virtue. Self-love becomes self-mastery when Virtue becomes your customary standard of behavior. You are worth committing to your highest self. Make You the priority.

Faith is believing in the unseen, knowing there's more to your power than what meets the eye. Your ego believes what it perceives. No matter how much your ego wants you to break a rule based on what you perceive as true, pause and wait for direction. Having faith is to know there is a Virtue available to extinguish a broken rule. The rules are left brain reactions while the pieces/Virtues are right brain responses. Sarcasm is left brain; fear and insecurity, humor is right brain; Faith and Tolerance. Lying is fear-based, left brain, while Integrity is Faith- based in the right brain. Avoid hurting your player by not allowing sarcasm to slip through your lips. He will know that you are not to be trusted.

When you are tempted to defend yourself, the move is to Acknowledge and Accept. This is not to say that you will accept the accusation as true, but rather, you accept the accusation as your player's truth. In the following moves, you will ask questions to gain an understanding about how they came to their conclusion. The more you keep your mind on The Game, the more you will see how there's a Virtue to counter every rule. In the beginning, it is common to feel lost without a move. With careful attention, you will start to see many imperfections in your behavior as well as in others. You might be tempted to think The Game's standard is ridiculously unattainable. Be careful, it's just another excuse to serve the Ego (devil). The defeated mindset is common among those who have not yet worked on their personal development. The Game is for the uncommon player who is ready to accept the challenge and rise to the level of self-actualization.

The player who is called to elevate knows he is perfect in the light of God but is restrained by the imperfection of the ego-mind contained within the physical existence. To love thyself is to love your one and only God with all your heart, and all your soul, and all your mind. To be virtuous is to be one with all that is good and true. Read, ask, and pray with all your heart for the Holy Spirit to give you Divine Understanding. Keep Love close and remember your motivation. Keep your standard of behavior high without making allowances. To make allowances after you've been given instruction will set yourself back again. Each time an allowance is made, you sacrifice your favor. Hold your conviction to maintain your seat in the tower. Make a commitment to *be* love, *one* with love, and the *guardian* for love. Honor God by choosing Love in *all* you do.

When you choose Love in all you do, you increase your self-awareness, become accountable to your perspective, attitude, and behavior. You know that your player is never responsible for your move; it's all on you. When you become consciously competent with your Virtues (knowing what to do *when you think* about it), you will be able to move through your circumstances quicker. With constant attention, you'll realize what to do or what not do with confidence. Choose the right move, know you are supernaturally protected by the power of God's promise to command his Angels where you are concerned, Psalm 91:11, and if you stick with it, you will be given authority over the nations, Revelation 2:26. *To master The Game,* you must become *unconsciously competent* with each move being second nature without thinking about it.

If you feel resistance with the philosophy of The Game, it means that your Queen is currently off the board. If you want to experience favor, it's imperative that you start believing The Game has merit. When you're operating from a place of self-doubt, not believing that your behavior will make such an enormous difference in your life, you will be more inclined to keep doing what you've always done. Without Faith, your need for control will drive you straight to Game Over. That's how fast The Game plays. Without your Virtues your responses will be a list of broken rules. The moment you hurt your player; Trust is lost. Game Over.

Master your pieces. Be respectful toward your player at all times. Each piece you master will expose the missing pieces from your player's side of the board. Use precaution before judging a move you've yet to witness. Be careful when you find your player physically attractive; if your board isn't stacked with pieces you could move too fast and lose the game. Never presume you are good enough, as the devil will slip in and steal your game in one stupid move. Be the watcher of self, not just your player. Slow the game down as it allows the universe to intervene and show you what you're missing. No need to worry about your player's character. You will recognize the worthiness of a lover, friend, business partner, superior, neighbor, or acquaintance again.

Virtue is your key (chi or energy) to peace, power, joy, wealth, happiness, purpose and destiny.

Therefore, anyone who breaks one of the least of these Commandments and teaches others accordingly will be called least in the Kingdom of Heaven, but whoever practices and teaches these commands will be called great in the Kingdom of Heaven.
For I tell you that unless your righteousness surpasses that of the Pharisees and the teachers of the law you will certainly not enter the Kingdom of Heaven.

Matthew 5:19-20

Do not teach others to act contrary to Love or you will be least in heaven. Be wise. Model well.

THE GREATEST COMMANDMENT

"Love the Lord your God with all your heart and with all your soul
and with all your mind. This is the first and greatest commandment.
And second is like it: Love your neighbor as yourself.
All the law and the Prophets hang on these two commandments."

Matthew 22:37-40

To love your God is to love yourself. Self-discipline—adjust your behavior. To love yourself with all your heart, soul, and mind. Second is to love your neighbor. That's the order. You first, then your player. Do not reverse the order.

LOVE FOR THE DAY IS NEAR

"Let no debt remain outstanding, except the continuing debt to
love one another for he who loves his fellow man has fulfilled the law."

Romans 13:8

Our purpose is to love one another to fulfill the law.

THE CHILDREN OF ABRAHAM

"If you hold to my teaching, you are really my disciples.
Then you will know the truth, and the truth will set you free."

John 8:31-3

Where there is a rule broken, there is a piece (Virtue) missing. A skilled player will honor the rules without exception, knowing that all of his answers lie within the pieces on the board. The following plays will help you shift your communication from ego to love.

Part 10

THE PLAYS

The fast track to polishing your game.

The plays give insight to how to correct the move. Notice if you fall toward the "DO NOT" list. Work to correct your understanding to apply the "DO" list to help you with your progress. Remember, the goal is to learn *how* to be *love* by recognizing and modifying your language and behavior. The plays will make sense—some you will inherently know, while others will help you see the nuance in communication.

1. **Do not distract your player with unnecessary communication while waiting for their move.** To know your player, you must watch in silence without influence. This is how you understand how they think and what's in their heart. Imagine the board. You wouldn't redirect your player's attention with your own idea about how to play his game; that would be imposing. Watch without interference. It will take Patience and Tolerance to watch your player and not say a thing.

2. **Do not succumb to threats by your player. Recognize his/her fear is being projected onto you to try and influence your move.** Example: "Well if you go out with that girl, everyone is going to think you're a fool." Meanwhile, she has a crush on you and is hoping to steer you away from her competition. Threats are a form of manipulation which is not allowed.

3. **Do not combine an occasion, especially a gift giving occasion (birthday, holiday, or anniversary) with an agenda to make amends.** Keep these separate. Consider carefully and be the watcher. Your gift although given in love, represents money. Don't buy her/ his love or forgiveness. Make amends prior to giving anything that requires a money exchange. Honor love before money.

4. **Do not sacrifice your values to ease the pain of your player's heart.** You will suffer negative consequences when you sacrifice yourself in attempt to spare your player.

5. **Do love yourself first by knowing and honoring your standard.** Keep your faith—your Queen, your relationship with God—first.

6. **Do not challenge your player.** The very word means to provoke. Love does not provoke or invite division.

7. **Do Acknowledge and Accept your player's move, rather than challenge them as to why they made it.** Seek to understand rather than to be right in your assumption. Example: your employee is late for work because he partied all night. It's best to recognize his choice of behavior (his move) rather than to challenge his decision and expect him to be different next time. Your game is not to change others; your game is to improve yourself.

8. **Do not self-promote.** Do not mention of your talents, skills, humor, knowledge, degrees, gifts, etc. "I'm so funny. I'm a great dancer. I can build a house by myself."

9. **Do let your player discover your talents as you play.** No need to show all your cards.

10. **Do not assume people want to give you their time.** Recognize when your player is graciously giving you their time and attention by listening to your stories, complaints, and drama—specifically, information that does not involve them. To be oblivious is to drain life force energy from your player, which pushes love away. Their

interaction and involvement of play with you will diminish until it's gone.

11. **Do remember to give your player a turn to respond after each of your points.** Speak and pause. Speak and pause. You can only make one move (statement or point) at a time. Pay attention to body language and level of interest. Are they asking questions? Are they involved or being polite? Honor their lack of interest and stop talking.

12. **Do not suggest an activity with an expectation for your player to oblige.** Your player is not obligated to accept any point of interest you may suggest. Don't get offended.

    "Hey, let's go bowling!"
    "No, I don't feel like it."

    Acknowledge and Accept the answer. If you are always the one to make suggestions and get denied, it's important to recognize the behavior, which is a lack of interest from your player than to make a point about how you feel. If you accuse your player of not caring about you or your interests, you set them up for defense.

13. **Do not put your player on defense by accusing or you will be at fault for prompting a defense.** Best to be the watcher to determine whether their lack of interest is in you or if it's a lack of interest in themselves. Your patience will polish your discernment.

14. **Do suggest your desired activity then pause for your player's interest.** Suggestion is your move; then wait, it's now their move. Practice patience while waiting for their move. If no response is made, honor the non-response, pivot, and do what makes you happy.

    "I feel like bowling. Do you want to come?"
    "No, I don't feel like it."
    "Okay, I'll see you later."

    If your player doesn't accept your suggestion, recognize the move. Be careful not to expect an immediate response. Your player may be exercising a pause while contemplating the answer. Be patient. Avoid accusing your player with an assumption, inadvertently positioning yourself to be blamed.

15. **Do not allow a woman to pay in public.** Period. Money is a tool of exchange for goods and services; it's not a barometer for equality, love, competence or fairness. The hierarchy of honor is for a man to lead and a woman to be cared for. If she must pay, plan prior to paying in public. Keep your financial business private. It is a man's honor to lead a spouse, business partner, friend, or acquaintance. Never quarrel over a bill in public. Be respectable. All money matters are to be handled privately. Relationship comes first.

16. **Do not laugh at your own jokes when no one else is laughing.** Laughter stimulates laughter, but you shouldn't be the only one laughing and certainly not laughing the loudest. Pay attention to your audience, their move is to laugh or not laugh. This will lead your response. Either move on or enjoy their laughter.

17. **Do not take yourself so seriously.** Laugh at your ignorance, mistakes, and self-discovery. (Adorable)

18. **Do not demean your player by name calling, swearing, revealing confidential information or humiliating in public.** These behaviors will result in an immediate loss of your King, not only to your player but to spectators as well. Consider carefully for even the most innocent moves can cause Game Over. Negligent banter like, "You idiot" "You're so fucking stupid" "I'm not the one who got an STD from my ex" and including behaviors like passing gas, burping, yelling, spitting, or making derogatory comments like "She may not be the prettiest of the bunch, but she's a good time" are completely prohibited. These may appear to be obviously disrespectful, but the same is true with comments said in jest or without self-awareness. "No, I don't participate. I just write the check." The moment you hurt someone directly or indirectly, you've lost their trust. Once trust is lost, it's Game Over.

19. **Do exercise the pause, hold your tongue, and think about how your player will receive your words before making a move.**

   Your intended sentiment holds little value compared to the actual words you choose. If you have to overexplain or defend your move, it was the wrong move. Apologies are meaningless when there's no change in behavior. Take your time to consider the virtue you will exercise, instead of reacting with a broken rule (sarcasm, accusation, defense).

20. **Do not annoy, be unkind, disrespect, or hate.** To annoy is to insist, persist, disregard, or show a lack of respect or self-respect. To be unkind is to lack empathy and speak hurtful words unnecessarily. To disrespect is to ignore the rules and continue to behave without virtue. Hate stems from judgment. Judgment stems from insecurity, and insecurity stems from a lack of self-worth. Hate is the outward behavior from the inward pain of low self-worth

21. **Do not react with anger, disdain, or consequence toward the villain before showing love toward the victim.**

22. **Do love the victim first.** Think of a car accident. Medics tend to the injured before focusing on who is at fault or cleaning up the mess. The same is true between players. Love first.

23. **Do not impose your ideas, stories, details or solutions onto your player without first having an invitation to do so, or before asking if you may.** To assume permission could offend your player and lead to their defense. Be careful to let your player respond to your move. Slow down and make one complete thought at a time. Your patience will ensure a clear and intentional conversation without back tracking because of assumptions or misunderstandings.

24. **Do recognize the problem, dilemma, or opportunity, and pause to see if your player is welcoming you to share or if the soil is ready for the seed.**

25.   **Do not feed insecurity in your partner.** Consider your wife's enchiladas. They aren't as good as your mom's. Instead of pointing out the truth, hurting your wife's feelings, *acknowledge* her effort and *accept* how delicious they are *graciously*. If she makes the statement, "They're not as good as your mom's," where she's looking for reassurance your reply should be, "Really, I think they're delicious." If her response is, "I don't think they're as good as your mom's, something is missing." She admits something is missing but can't figure it out. That's your invitation for a suggestion. Your reply is, "I don't know, but I think she… (insert suggestion)." Pay attention to her move and respond accordingly. Do not confirm her insecurity by saying, "I love my mom's enchiladas. They are my favorite." Although your confirmation may be the truth, it's unnecessary. Your move could hurt your wife and your truth could cost you her trust.

26.   **Do offer suggestions when there's an open forum in a group setting.** Pause, be the watcher, determine if the table is open for suggestions. If so, be *patient* to fully understand others before offering advice. It's important for you to recognize your player. There will be plenty of time for others to get to know you.

27.   **Do not give unsolicited advice.** No matter how simple the solution. It will fall on deaf ears. It's not your job to solve your player's problem, or make their move, especially when they're not asking for your help. Avoid having your intelligence insulted should your player disregard your advice. Parents are often guilty of unsolicited advice. Learn to turn the table by waiting to be asked. In doing so, your advice will be respected instead of ignored. Better to have an inquiry than to impose on your player's side of the board.

28.   **Do not waste your pearls on swine.** Be careful not to give the best of your time, talent, money, hospitality, and grace to those who don't appreciate you. Maintain your value by playing with admirable players.

29. **Do not lie.** One untruth makes every move questionable. White lies, dirty lies, small and big—once a lie leaves your lips, trust is lost. It's Game Over as the universe exposes the truth. To your player, a liar may be tolerated, but a liar is never trusted. Opportunities come to an end when trust is off the board. Never call out a lie that's been discovered. It's better to see your player's game than to make known what can be denied. When you offer your player a chance to defend themselves against a lie you are offering an unspoken contract of acceptance. Which means you are willing to lower your standards, accept their reason or apology for lying, forgive them and continue the game. Unfortunately, there is no game because the King is lost. To continue playing means you have self-sacrificed, as lying has now become the new standard. The standard will be played repeatedly until the inevitable end. Game Over.

30. **Do have self-awareness. How's your demeanor?** When you discover a lie, your move will depend on your relationship with your player. When a child lies, the move is compassion because he's acting in fear. A lover requires grace to maintain your self-respect. A friend requires mercy because of their insecurity about the truth, and diplomacy for you to effectively push away from the board.

31. **Do not put your player in a position to make a decision that should be made by you.** Deflecting your responsibility onto another is a weakness in character and conviction as you inherently know the right move to make, but you don't want to make it, so you relinquish your responsibility to your player. Should they make the wrong decision, you remain faultless. Now you have someone to blame. That's weak. Let's consider. A girl wants to go to a party where there will be boys. Her boyfriend is not going. She wants to go but is struggling with her decision because she knows it's not right by him. She asks her boyfriend if she should go to the party. This gives her the advantage as he is torn, between what he wants to say what she wants him to say. It is not his decision to make. It's a dishonorable move for her to put him

in the position. The right move is to reflect as if the roles were reversed. She would expect him to make the honorable decision without her influence.

32. **Do not ask to borrow items from your player knowing they are particular about the item.** You will be the cause of a dilemma, making your player choose between the love of you and the love of self, which could easily be mistaken for the love of money (material before relationship). Honor your relationship by respecting your player's belongings. No one is entitled to another man's possessions. (Respect).

33. **Do be respectful with other peoples' belongings.** Stop to consider the material and sentimental value before imposing your prerogative to take what you want.

34. **Do not talk about dysfunctional friends and family in public or any gathering.** Gossiping about others is dishonorable in any setting, but in public you run the risk of losing your King with your spectators.

35. **Do not talk about your 'woe-is-me' stories regarding past experiences where you've been wronged.** There are always two sides to every story; your side will only make you look bad and expose your pain. People will judge you by your words, not your injustice. Stay in honor, no complaining.

36. **Do celebrate people in your presence and those who are not. Edification is a skill that everyone loves and appreciates.** The universe and your player will look favorably upon you.

37. **Do not make excuses.** Period. Not for being late, not for hurtful words, failed actions, wrong actions, for the lack of funds or anything. Find a positive way to move on without excuses. It is better to remain silent, than to make an excuse. The reason we make excuses is because we know we've failed someone somewhere somehow. The remedy is to change your perspective from meeting other peoples' expectations to the reality of your chosen actions. You don't need to explain yourself. It is what it is, do or do not, and move on.

38. **Do or Do not; there is no try.** Excuses are allowances you give yourself for your lack of accomplishment. Either you did it, or you did not do it. Own it.

39. **Do not blame others for your actions, words, decisions, results, or thought process.** When you look outside yourself, there will always be a reason to rationalize your behavior. Only you are responsible for your words, deeds, actions and thought process. If you don't like your results, slow down and reconsider before acting, in order to be fully confident with your move.

40. **Do take responsibility.** Apologize when the opportunity arises. Leadership is not about being right all the time. Leadership is about accountability and responsibility for yourself and others, whether right or wrong. The need for an apology will come with discernment. To be able to accept responsibility and apologize for a wrong move shows strength of character, not weakness.

41. **Do not take credit.** There's no need to verbalize your contribution to anyone as you will inadvertently take credit away from others. Whatever you do is between you and God. A job well done will be rewarded with favor from above regardless of recognition from others. Be patient and wait for your time of recognition. Humility is a virtue.

42. **Do listen for acknowledgment.** People are messengers. When you have done a good job in the eyes of God, his approval will be heard through the voices around you.

43. **Do not make assumptions.** Be very cautious. Assumptions are hidden in limiting beliefs, preconceived ideas, education, expectations, environment, arrogance, entitlement, percept-ions, social acceptance, politics, race, ignorance, and various human behaviors. Assumptions are accepted conclusions based on past experience or presumed knowledge. To avoid making assumptions, you must stay present and only operate with present facts. The Game allows only one move at a time for each player. To *assume* would be to make a move based

on what you believe your player's next two moves or more would be. Stop playing ahead of the present move. Your assumptions will begin to dissolve when you've grown to recognize the difference between a virtue and a rule in your player. When you've stopped making assumptions before making a move, you're on your way to mastering The Game. Self-mastery takes time. It's simple but not easy.

44. **Do ask for clarity.** People struggle to convey their intent with clarity because they use the incorrect order of words, incorrect definition, and analogies to express their thoughts and desires. Keep in mind that very few people can articulate clearly from the heart. For example, how often do you hear someone say, "That's not what I meant to say." Somehow, humanity has adopted a language where it is difficult to say what we mean, so we talk in code expecting others to read between the lines. Don't assume, ask for clarification.

45. **Do not boast about your accolades by name dropping or sharing your association or experience as a precursor for respect.** Do not talk about yourself or your skill set until it becomes relevant. Save yourself from breaking the no boasting rule. Be humble. Keep your knowledge, gifts, and talents in your pocket until you're called to reveal them.

46. **Do allow for your behavior, knowledge, and demeanor to earn respect.** Let your player discover who you are. If you are all that, your player will recognize and tell you who you are. Be humble.

47. **Do not attempt to gain interest from your player by buying unsolicited gifts.** Never use money as a way to gain attention or get people to like you. A person of value will not appreciate the insult to their character as they cannot be bought. Buying someone's affection or attention will reflect a lack of personal value. A shallow investment brings shallow returns. If you buy a stranger a drink at the bar, you're using a material item to do your fishing for you, like bait on a pole. It's better to have the courage and confidence to walk up and say, "Hello."

48. **Do be generous with thoughtful gifts—material, sentimental, and intangible with unconditional love.** To love harder is to push yourself to give unconditionally, rather than strive for personal gain.

49. **Do not force your pursuit upon your player and expect a return of interest.** If you are not receiving a mutual response according to your advancement, Acknowledge and Accept that you're not a match for your player. People will naturally gravitate to each other when interested, but not always for the same reasons. Use discernment to understand the attraction.

50. **Do not feel you need to prematurely disclose your personal information or past in the name of honesty and disclosure.** Everyone experiences loss, a failed relationship, and decisions and situations in life they're not proud of. There's no need to share all your past with your player before it's necessary. Your history is irrelevant unless its discovery could cost you your King. Be wise to know the difference. Stay focused on the present to prove your character rather than explaining your past behavior.

51. **Do be truthful. If someone asks about your past, and it feels like an intrusion, recognize their sense of entitlement.** You *need not* answer according to their expectation but do be truthful with your answer. "How long has it been since you had sex?" is an irrelevant and presumptuous question that need not be answered according to expectation. Their anticipated response would serve as a cause for judgment, imposed by their entitlement to your personal business. The best answer is to be truthful about their inquiry. "Why are you asking me this question?" Notice the diplomacy in the move. I did not say, "I don't know, why do you ask?" This means, "I'll answer dependent upon your answer." This answer indicates a lack of trust. A lack of trust means there's no King on the board. It's Game Over. The relationship will not be successful. To say, "Why are you asking me this question?" with sincere curiosity and without sounding offended,

is to be transparent and straightforward. It implies that you have a boundary.

Now, they are put in a position to explain their reasoning. Their next move is imperative. If the response is, "I don't know. Why, do you have something to hide?" or "Never mind, it's no big deal," your player is dismissing their lack of boundary, deflecting back to you without being accountable to your question. What's important for you to recognize is the move, not the circumstance. First, they made two moves by asking a question and not waiting for an answer, then they made a second move by making a statement for dismissal. They dismissed, crossed a boundary, deflected, and failed to be accountable. This is how you recognize your player. Regardless of content of the inquiry, your player will use those tactics again down the road. On the other hand, if their response is, "I'm curious because I haven't had sex in a while." They are playing by the rule of one move at a time, being truthful, authentic, and accountable to your inquiry, showing they are able to respond appropriately according to your question instead of responding to their assumption of inference. When you recognize entitlement, lack of boundary, deflecting, and no accountability in your player's behavior, the same character will hold true regardless of the circumstances.

52. **Do not be disagreeable, quick to challenge, or find reason to say no.** Those who are quick to say no and are naturally disagreeable or resistant, have trust issues. They lack faith in their ability to be vulnerable. Their behavior will prove to break all the rules which will cost them their King. The sooner you see it, the less time you'll invest in their game. Watch carefully.

53. **Do practice being agreeable before making a decision.** You will learn a lot more, be exposed to more opportunities, and be open for blessing when your vibration is in agreement. The universe operates in agreement. Even when you have to say 'no,' practice saying 'yes' first.

"Betty, would you like to go to lunch today?"
"I would love to go to lunch. Can we go on Friday instead?"

This is a far better answer than rejecting with an excuse.

"I'm sorry I can't. I have to clean my kitchen."

The first response acknowledges the invitation and accepts with an alternate plan. If you don't want to go at all, respond with, "Thank you, how about a rain check?" Bow out with grace.

54. **Do pay your debts.** When you owe borrowed money from friends, family, children, a boss, coworker or neighbor, always pay back the debt as soon as possible, even if it's in small increments. Never take your player for granted by assuming they don't care if you pay what you promised to return. To do so shows a lack of respect for your relationship, which is dishonorable behavior. Your player will lose trust in you; therefore, you have lost your King. Better to acknowledge the debt and pay as promised in order to maintain the relationship.

55. **Do exercise a sweet tongue for it can break a bone.** Proverbs 15:1 Even the most difficult player can be overcome when you know what to say and when to say it.

56. **Do care more about you and your well-being.** Take time for self-care. Enjoy an apple, go for a walk and listen to the birds, get a massage, play or listen to music, change your surroundings, sit on the beach, meditate. Your time is your own. You must participate in the quality of life you desire. No one else has the power to do so. Don't wait for "time" to schedule your special day. Time is an illusion. Your 'time' will never come unless you own it today. When you make time for self-care, The Game becomes much easier because you have the patience to slow down, think, and respond one move at a time.

57. **Do not follow another man's desires, opinions, or demands without first considering your own.** Look at the board. Your player makes a move, and it's your turn to respond. Acknowledge and Accept the suggestion with grace. It's Friday night. Your coworker wants to go out. You want to go home.

"Come on, I'm bored, please?"

"I hear you (acknowledge). I feel that way too sometimes (accept). But I'm going home, be safe."

There's no reason to submit to guilt. No self-sacrifice.

58.   **Do be like a reed in the wind.** Be flexible. Be easy going, agreeable, and open to suggestion without taking offense. Be careful not to get upset when your desire, expectation, or suggestion is vetoed for an alternate plan. If you suggest a movie to your group, and they decide on something else, don't take offense. It's a decision, not a conspiracy. If your family wants pizza and not the dinner you made, don't take offense. Go with the flow, make it easy, and wrap up the dinner for tomorrow. Now you have free time.

59.   **Do not become complacent with your routine.** To have faith on the board, you must have an unattainable vision for your life. Something from the heart, where you have no idea how to get there. The magic and beauty in this experience comes when you're free to play. Playful is lighthearted, humorous, joyful, creative, and silly. A child explores his world with curiosity in the present moment. Be curious. Move, dance, sing, discover, open your arms to receive. Life is a gift, open it.

60.   **Do not combine a gift with an agenda.** If you give an offering at the same time you ask for a favor, your offer appears as a bribe. Instead, be transparent with your need, allowing your player to accept or deny unconditionally. If your player agrees to help you, you can then show your appreciation when the opportunity arises (you can create the opportunity.)

61.   **Do give from the heart without condition.** Never expect anything in return.

62.   **Do not bulldoze or place blame.** If you have first-hand knowledge of the truth, ask questions. Refrain from imposing your internal dialogue into the conversation.

63. **Do wait to speak.** Be humble by showing interest in your player rather than being more interested in your player knowing you.

64. **Do not attempt to teach by combining the opportunity to boast about your own life, experiences, and skills when your player asks for advice.** Keep your advice focused on their remedy, not your life story.

65. **Do lead by affirming your player's skills and affirming what you see in him or another.** Edification is a wonderful skillset that benefits both players.

66. **Do not worry.** Worry is for the one who fears. Check yourself when you start to worry. Take a look at your immediate circumstances. Most worries are about the future. Have faith and continue to behave in the present. Be confident that you'll know your answer when you need it.

67. **Do live in the now.** Your present moment requires you to respond to your circumstances. Your future depends on how you play in the present moment. There's nothing to worry about in the future if you continue to play in the present moment. Believe everything will work out to your benefit.

68. **Do not allow your mind to control you with future fears of "what if."** This will only cause you to lose control of your game in the present moment. Your emotions will have you breaking the rules because your Queen is off the board. When you find yourself trying to base your move on "what if" speculations, know that you are trying to play both sides of the board, indicative of a false sense of control. The only control you have is to make your move according to your pieces.

69. **Do stay focused on the relationships you want to keep.** You must hold a vision of what you want to experience. Healthy relationships are the key to a beautiful life. Focus on your vision. Believe that you can have it. The key is to sharpen the detail of your vision, feel it within your soul, then love your way to it. The faster you can substitute rules with virtue, the faster your dream will be realized.

70. **Do not attach yourself to circumstances.** Circumstances serve as the barrier to what you want, but it's an illusion. Don't be fooled by what you see with your eyes. Focus your mind's eye on what you want. Detach from everything that does not serve your vision.

71. **Do own your move.** Be accountable and aware when it's your time to move. Recognize when the move is not yours. Stay on your side of the board. Don't be tempted to manage your player's side. You'll be doing yourself a disservice.

72. **Do not tell people how to live their lives.** This is imposing and assumes entitlement. Recognize when you're telling others what to do. Even with children. Let go of your need to control others. You'll have a move, when your player calls you to the table.

73. **Do build your own life.** Focus on your own character, dreams, aspirations, and education without comparing yourself to others. Your life is between you and God.

74. **Do not tell people what you're going to do or how you'll do it.** This gives ammunition for their doubt, negativity, gossip, and blame should you not produce according to their expectation. Protect your honor and integrity by not sharing your plans or ideas with spectators. You are free to make changes to your plan without permission. Your King is safe.

75. **Do what you're going to do.** Just do it. You don't need permission or validation to fulfill your desires. Believe in your dream and move toward it one move at a time.

76. **Do remember everything is in divine timing, just keep moving.** Soon the puzzle will start to come together, and all will make sense. Follow your counselor - intuition.

77. **Do not attempt to answer an implication or insinuation.** In other words, don't read into a message, just read the message. "Oh, you look nice today," doesn't mean you don't look nice on other days. It simply means you look nice. The proper response is, "Thank you." Do not ask

for clarity as if the compliment was underhanded. Acknowledge and Accept.

78. **Do answer the words exactly as they are presented without inferring or making allowances for what your player meant to say.** When your player says, "Oh, I don't have anything to do this weekend," and you understand that's your queue for an invitation, don't be guilted into filling their calendar. Ask a question. "Why don't you have anything to do this weekend?" This is a perfectly acceptable response if you have no interest in being in their company. Acknowledge and Accept with an innocent question. When they answer with, "I don't have anyone to go out with," you respond with, "I'm sorry. I'm sure something will come up." Again, you Acknowledge and Accept what is being said rather than avoiding the issue by changing the subject or caving under pressure.

Your player may get annoyed, because clearly, you're not picking up what they are throwing down. Your player might challenge your ignorance by imposing their will upon you with another question.

"What are you doing this weekend? Do you want to hang out?"

Remember, no excuses. You don't need a reason for why you don't want to visit. Clearly, she didn't pick up on your lack of interest, and now she feels entitled to know your business. Watch your player's moves to see what rules she's breaking. Keep your answer authentic, short and to the point. "I don't know yet," is good enough. That tells your player you're not interested in joining her. If she continues with a suggestion, and you are still not interested, you simply say,

"Maybe, I'll let you know how I'm feeling."

79. **Do not over explain.** It's not necessary to give multiple analogies and references to prove your point, assuming your player doesn't understand you. Speak concisely, that's your move. Be confident that your player will ask for further clarification if needed. Only then can you reiterate with simplicity and allow your player to make their

move. Acknowledge and Accept that he will either understand you, ask questions, or not understand, or not care to understand. Whatever it is, that's his move. Be patient to let him make his move, however long it takes. If he doesn't ask further questions or have a relevant comment, your move is to change the subject.

80. **Do not make accusations based on assumptions.** "What do you mean you just ate? Now, you're not going to be hungry for the dinner I spent all day making." Instead, ask a question. "Are you going to want dinner, or should I save it for tomorrow?" Remember, don't get offended and don't be defensive. Your player's decision to eat doesn't hurt you. However, if the move was a lack of consideration because he ate right before dinner without telling you and failed to offer to bring you something, then his King is in danger as your Trust in him becomes threatened.

81. **Do ask questions when accused.** Regardless of the absurdity of the accusation, do not defend yourself. Instead, seek understanding by acknowledging what is being said and accepting the emotion behind the accusation. Ask questions to gain clarity but be careful not to ask accusatory questions. Otherwise, you are guilty of behaving in a demeaning way which can be considered bullying.

82. **Do not ask direct questions based on suspicion.** "Where were you last night? I didn't see your car." This inquiry is intrusive as it implies deception and will rarely be answered genuinely. If you have a suspicion, the correct move is to become the watcher. A deceptive player always leaves clues. You need not know the truth. The moment you don't trust your player, Game Over.

83. **Do watch your words and actions.** Your player consistently communicates. Oftentimes, words and actions fail to align. Don't assume the definition is a lack of integrity. Sometimes, big words precede little action, big actions have no words, and actions don't follow the words spoken. Discernment is a Virtue.

84. **Do not defend yourself.** There will be no excuses, reasons, or unsolicited information. You don't owe an explanation. You are accountable to God. When your actions align with Honor and Integrity, your words need not be present.

85. **Do not make negative assumptions based on insecurities.** You don't feel pretty enough, so you assume your player is attracted to other women. You don't have a degree, so you assume you're not good enough instead of being confident with who you are.

86. **Do practice being the watcher of self.** Ask yourself, why do I feel this way? Self-analysis is key. Am I insecure, making assumptions, or have I lost trust? Where is my issue?

87. **Do not be needy.** To be needy is a clear indication of a lack of self-love. No one can give you what you need until you fulfill your needs for yourself. Once you learn self-love, you're no longer dependent on another for your happiness. Now, you're ready to love another.

88. **Do work to fill your own cup by giving yourself what you need to build self-confidence.** Self-educate according to your interests. Ask for spiritual guidance during your silence. Decide to be of impeccable character in all you do. Whatever your occupation; success will follow you.

89. **Do not make money references in public (i.e., income, possessions, investments, flashing a wallet).** The moment you let the material world speak for you, you're breaking the rule of boasting. Stay humble.

90. **Do manage your money prior to going out to ensure a respectful evening.** Never go unprepared, allowing others to cover for you. Honor never takes advantage of anyone, especially women.

91. **Do not show disrespect toward others by disrespecting yourself.** Show up confident in your ability to be a team player. Know that you're seen by everyone, even when you feel small and insignificant. Watch your language.

92. **Do remember to protect your Queen and King.** Dishonorable behavior will ensue when you forget to believe in your purpose to love. To protect your King, learn to keep your mouth shut by having faith that the Truth will always come to light.

93. **Do not attempt to make more than one move at a time.** Choose your words, actions, and observations with care to avoid crossing your boundary. When you say too much you run the risk of making assumptions that lead to premature responses. Premature responses indicate more than one move has been made and will expose your fears, insecurities, and control issues. Patience is a Virtue.

94. **Do exercise Patience.** Most of the time you'll be by yourself, with your own thoughts. Don't waste energy trying to predict or draw your own conclusions. Have faith that all relevant facts will come to light when you're in play. There's no need to go looking for evidence or clues, interrogating innocent bystanders. Maintain self-respect by staying present in the moment.

95. **Do not expect to play equally with someone who doesn't know or understand The Game.** Heartbreak and disappointment are inevitable as your player's ignorance will continue to let you down. Those who lack self-awareness will unknowingly cause pain to you, themselves, and others. Be the watcher. Acknowledge and Accept.

96. **Do remember you have one turn to make one move.** Some moves require the use of multiple Virtues in one move or use one Virtue at a time in subsequent moves. Pause, remember you have another turn coming. No matter how long it takes, it's coming. Be patient. *Wait.*

97. **Do not rely on your senses (ears, eyes, and feelings), nor assume to understand your player before having a true understanding of The Game.** The Game is complex.

98. **Do pan back, observe and consider the whole board, with all the pieces, before making a move (taking action).** Is your Virtue present or are you about to break the rules? Pause to question yourself

before looking for fault in your player. Every move your player makes is an opportunity for you to correct your behavior to align with love.

99. **Do not change the direction of the conversation before acknowledging your player's move.** Accept what is being said without getting offended. When your player is condescending or insulting you, exercise patience by utilizing the pause, then ask for clarification if you find the move to be offensive. Be humble. Don't defend by challenging their intelligence, title, age, or importance. Don't allow your ego to defend, interrupt, or correct before it's your turn. Be careful to recognize when it's more important to let go. When in doubt, choose to be Love rather than to be right.

100. **Do have confidence in your abilities but remember to exercise humility.** When you know who you are, there's no need to tell others who you are. If it's true, your player will recognize you.

101. **Do not attempt to play your player's game.** Mind your own business. Stay on your side of the board. When you make the right move you'll see a favorable response returned.

102. **Do continue to focus on your pieces.** Each time you're frustrated, or you get angry, it's because you can't control your player. If you don't have a move to solve the issue, you're missing that Virtue.

103. **Do not disregard the weight of your player's words.** Pay close attention to the topic of conversation: people-events-ideas. The lowest vibrational players, the emotionally suffering, consume themselves with gossip. Next are those who consume themselves with events irrelevant to their life and behavior. Those with ideas, solutions, and valuable intellect should be carefully observed to identify them as a virtuous player. Be careful to discern between intellect and character. One does not assume the other. Name, title, stature, wealth, and reputation can be a veil to cover poor character. Listen carefully to recognize their pieces. If you make allowances for poor character in hopes of personal advancement, you'll be disappointed every time.

104. **Do not be pressured by time.** Time is an illusion. You have time. Start now. Stop making excuses. The idea of the past, or urgency of the future are all constructs of fear and control. You have all the time you need. Have Faith that everything arrives in God's perfect timing. Embrace your setbacks and delays.

105. **Do believe everything you need is here in the now.** Make your moves based on the current circumstances in the present moment. Do not make moves based on future predictions. A move made prematurely will require retracting.

106. **Do not assume your status, title, credit report, accolades, bank account, popularity or accomplishments will speak for your character.** These accomplishments work to support your Ego and say little about your behavior. This junk drawer supports the Ego—who we think we are. Don't be fooled. God sees through these worldly accomplishments. The proof of your character is in the magic of your experience. Accolades don't produce the extraordinary; only love can do that.

107. **Do not interrupt the overflow of your player's heart.** Listening without interruption gives you clarity and understanding for your correct move. Your accuracy will improve when you listen patiently for your turn.

108. **Do practice compassion.** Words give clues to underlying pain. The rules identify insecurities in your player. When you identify the insecurity, your move is to Acknowledge and Accept his emotional responses. Be humble, use compassion by choosing to understand your player without giving unsolicited advice. If an apology is needed, do not use the word 'if' in your apology. "I'm sorry *if* I hurt you." Or "I'm sorry *if* you got hurt." The correct way to apologize is to be accountable for their pain. "I'm sorry I hurt you." Allow your player to correct the record if you're not the cause. Ask, "have I hurt you?" The question implies that you care enough to understand, and humble enough not to defend when your tone is sincere.

109. **Do not use sarcastic questions as a defense.** "Oh, so that's what you think?" "Really, is that what you think I am?" Sarcasm tells your player you have an insecurity. Questions should allow you to gain clarity. Don't make your question an attack on your player.

110. **Do ask questions with an innocent curiosity to gain a greater understanding of your player's perspective.** Be careful not to word your question in a way that triggers a defensive response. When your player lacks a full understanding of the topic, your move is to be humble. Educate when asked and never humiliate.

111. **Do not get defensive.** When your player asks you challenging questions, be humble and authentic by admitting that you don't know, or simply say, "According to my understanding..." Leave room for your player to add to the conversation. To admit that you don't have a full understanding (even when you do) is endearing.

112. **Do not feel obligated to answer questions regarding your money or finances.** Your money is your business. Recognize when your player feels entitled to your privacy. Simply answer with, "I don't understand the relevance of your question?"

113. **Do be gracious to redirect the conversation with humor or ask a question to gain understanding.**

    His move: "How much money do you have?" (Consider the intimacy of your relationship with your player).
    Your move: "Why, who needs to know?"
    (humor) "Well, that depends on who's asking?"
    (question) "Where?"
    This one move sets the boundary to say, 'My money is not your money."
    His move: "C'mon man, I need some money."
    Your move: "What *do you need?*"

    Notice you didn't ask, "How much do you need?" You asked, *"What do you need?"* Not, "What do you need it *for?*" The first question implies consent. Asking what the money would be used for implies judgment before the budget approval. When you ask, "What do you need?" the honest inquiry affords you the opportunity to fulfill the need without involving money. How we pose our questions is the finesse behind The Game. Grace is knowing what to say and when to say it.

114. **Do not lend money.** If you allow your player to borrow money with the expectation for its return, you're setting yourself up for disappointment, anger, bullying, accusations, and the need to remind your player of his promise. A loan is contrary to Love. If your player asks for money, your charity extends to what you can afford to give without expecting a return. There's no need to agree or deny that your money is a loan. Allow your player to return the money or forget about it. Just remember that you're not keeping record; you are looking for the integrity of his word.

115. **Do give with an open hand without expectation from your player.** If your player has lost your trust, he should not be in a position to ask. Move from the table. Should your player promise to repay, his integrity is on the line. Do not remind him.

116. **Do not assume that the person you want to play with wants to play with you.** When you set your eyes on someone, don't chase them around imposing yourself to make them give you their attention. Look for consent by their attraction. If they are attracted, watch to see if they are attracted further than the first two gates.

117. **Do not give extended explanations for anything.** Be concise, there's no need for further clarification unless your player asks a question. Over explaining insults your player's intelligence while simultaneously conveying that you feel misunderstood. Over explaining is received as weakness. Move forward believing your point is understood. Remember, you are trying to recognize your player. Being understood is secondary.

118. **Do answer 'yes' or 'no.'** Give the simplest answer to be specific. Remember one move at a time. Allow your player to prompt your

next move. Avoid seeming flippant, uninterested, or ambiguous. "Yes, I would like that," or, "no, I've haven't seen that movie." The skillful conversationalist practices a respectful exchange.

119. **Do not volunteer information where there's been no inquiry.** Consider carefully before over sharing or you might "dump, bulldoze" or inadvertently lose your King. Is your information relevant? Will it help or hinder your player's understanding of you? Are you being prompted to over share by an imposing inquiry? Do you feel obligated? Are you defending yourself? Be cautious not to unnecessarily explain yourself. Explaining yourself to anyone will not be expected when your behavior aligns with Virtue. If your player doesn't understand your move, allow him to ask.

120. **Do wait for *direct* questions.** There's no need to answer insinuations.

    "Would you like diet or regular?"
    A direct question gets a direct answer. "Regular please."
    "They have diet too if you like." The assumed insinuation is that you could lose a few pounds, whether it was intentional or not. Acknowledge and Accept.
    "No thank you, regular is fine." There's no need to challenge your player's intent in their question. Let it go.

121. **Do not show your hand.** If you feel compelled to share your thoughts, or offer irrelevant information to your player, pause. Be careful what thought processes, plans, judgments, and decision-making strategies you reveal. Ask yourself why you're considering sharing. Is it necessary? What will the information invite?

122. **Do let your player's curiosity about you lead the way for conversation.** Be patient when sharing your talents and life story. If your player isn't asking, accept the lack of interest. If you lack self-awareness, you'll impose on your player's time. Patience allows your players interest in you to grow.

123. **Do not point out your player's flaws, shortcomings, or differences, especially in public.** The move is hurtful, disrespectful, and unnecessary. Hurt your player, Trust is gone. Game Over.

124. **Do be tolerant.** Recognize poor behavior as an example of what not to do.

125. **Do not support your argument with past experience to prove your point.** Stay present. Once you bring up the past, you invite your player to do the same. Avoid arguments by responding to what is current and relevant to the present.

126. **Do have faith in a solution.** When your player makes a move toward blaming or making excuses, keep the conversation respectful by staying away from defending or challenging his excuses. Pause. If the correct move isn't apparent, let your faith (Queen) take the lead. Wait to let the universe give you direction. There's no need to rush your response. Use the pause especially when angry. Hold your tongue. Let the wave of emotion pass over you until you can think clearly.

127. **Do not feel obligated to answer your player's intrusive questions.** It's easy to be offended and tempted to defend yourself, but don't cross your boundary. "How much does your dad make a year?" is an intrusive question. Your dad's income is his business, not to be shared by or with anyone. A simple response could be, "None, my mom does all the cooking." If you do not assume to understand the meaning of his question, you have more options for the answer. Take the opportunity to misunderstand the question. Don't be afraid to look stupid. When others assume your ignorance, you're in control. If your player asks again by clarifying the question, answer directly by saying, "I don't understand the question." Allow yourself to be perceived as ignorant. In many cases, ignorance is your best friend. Ignorance allows your player to feel superior and safe. When your player feels safe, his heart will be revealed.

128. **Do take advantage of inserting a humorous diversion.** As your humor piece becomes more polished, your responses become more lighthearted without humiliation or sarcasm.

129. **Do not disregard your disrespectful behavior toward your player after you have cooled down.** Be accountable to your actions and apologize with a sincere heart. A prompt apology can save your King.

130. **Do apologize relevant to your part of the argument without blaming your player or making excuses for your words.** Do not expect to be forgiven.

131. **Do listen to your player's method of operation.** Is he pulling rank to support his argument? Is he challenging your knowledge by asking for proof or references? Recognize that your player is feeling threatened. Hold the pause.

132. **Do exercise patience when you suspect deception, become the watcher.** The Truth will be told without your interference.

133. **Do not phone your player and unload your emotions.** Be respectful and ask if you are interrupting something before continuing.

134. **Do be respectful.** Give your player the opportunity to accept or reject. Listen carefully to discern if your player is reluctantly compliant or open for conversation.

135. **Do use discernment when invited to attend a function.**

    Personal invite or general?
    Fundraiser or birthday party?
    Intimate or gala?

    Relationships always come first. If it's a personal invite for a semi-intimate birthday celebration, the answer is 'yes.' Make it happen. If they love you enough to invite you, love them enough to attend. General invitations are at your discretion. Should you commit, keep your word and show up.

136. **Do not try to establish common ground with your player by admission of guilt.** The move will prematurely reduce your value.

137. **Do communicate what is relevant.** Withholding irrelevant information about your past is not secrecy, its discernment. Wait until it becomes relevant.

138. **Do not be negative or contrary about the desires of your player's heart.** Let them enjoy their journey with excitement and pride in that moment. If you hinder their enthusiasm, you will lose their trust. Wait for the invitation to give an alternate view and be careful not to challenge your player's vision. Listen and ask questions.

139. **Do not use fear to manipulate your desired result.** The moment you choose to manipulate, you push Love away.

140. **Do be true to yourself.** Know there's a higher power, working to bring your desire. Your player serves as the opportunity to prove your commitment.

141. **Do not make excuses as to why you can't love someone because they don't love you back.** Love is unconditional. Never put conditions or expectations for a return of love as a barrier to your virtuous behavior. Sex and love are not interdependent. To love is spiritual; sex is physical. Spiritual love needs no consent, where physical love does. To love, at its foundation , means I will not hurt you.

142. **Do be mindful to be respectful, kind, and gracious.** Remain loyal to yourself with everyone; be the same with a player who's lost their King. Should they come into your space, remember you're in play with the universe. A respectful demeanor is not an invitation for your player to re-establish the relationship.

143. **Do not make sexual comments, innuendos, or advancements toward your player.** The move is demeaning and conveys you're not respectable nor respectful. Sexual connotations devalue yourself and your player. The lack of self-respect and personal boundary is

an automatic loss of a King. A player without boundary is not to be trusted in any circumstance.

144. **Do not tolerate a player who makes hints or innuendos about their sexual desire or intent with you.** Their lack of respect gives evidence about your relationship moving forward. When your player demonstrates who they are, believe them the first time. Disrespectful behavior will be magnified, not diminished, over time.

145. **Do recognize the humble player who is hesitant to ask for help.** The move is to offer contribution.

146. **Do use diplomacy when your player's motive becomes apparent.** Don't be openly offended and call him out. It's time to be the watcher. It's not game over until he makes the final move to lose your trust. Do not interfere, make assumptions, speculations, or accusations.

147. **Do not hesitate to contact your player if they haven't contacted you.** To love is to follow your heart. However, be careful not to impose your will, ignoring the boundary set by your player. If your player doesn't show the same care for you, Acknowledge and Accept. Maintain honorable behavior by being respectful of their position.

148. **Do follow your intuition.** If your heart is leading you, follow. It's always the right move when the King is on the board. It's important to know the difference between a selfish move and an unconditional act of love. If the move is self-serving, you will be disappointed when your expectations bring consequence instead of blessing.

149. **Do not disrespect or demean a child by accusing him of being something that he isn't.** In other words, no name calling. Be careful of the words you plant in his subconscious. Think about what you would like to see come to fruition instead of destroying your child with fearful predictions. You're accountable for his self-worth and esteem as the steward for God's creation.

150. **Do be a role model for loving behavior.** Demonstrate what love looks like by operating in virtue. Be patient and kind. Have mercy on the child's soul. See the future adult you wish to see in him and act accordingly. Someday, the child will look back on your behavior. Your present behavior sets the foundation for future appreciation.

151. **Do not presume to be funny.** Be humble with your humor. Pay attention to your player to see if they laugh. A courtesy laugh is different from a real laugh that makes everyone laugh together.

152. **Do not condemn your player's effort, no matter the quality.** His effort can be improved upon with encouragement. Find a way to show appreciation.

153. **Do lighten up on the seriousness of the job being performed to preserve the relationship.** Show compassion for your player's incompetence, while having faith in their growth. Your loving acceptance is more important than your expectation for their standard. Learn to play and be light-hearted. If the situation is not life threatening, it's not that serious.

154. **Do not *impose* affection or attention on your player when problems arise in your relationship.** Give your player time to Acknowledge and Accept your lighthearted perspective. Your player may not feel the same as you do, and will result in them feeling not heard or respected. You will lose your King.

155. **Do distinguish the difference between the problem and your player.** Direct your anger toward the problem and not your player. If you feel that your player is the problem, it means you've lost respect for them. The game has ended.

156. **Do not assume pet names like 'sweetheart, darling, hon, babe' are okay with your player.** The relationship may not be appropriate. Do not proceed without consent. The lack of respect and respectable behavior will push love away. It's game over.

157. **Do use first names, and when appropriate, address by their last name.** No 'Hey' or 'Hey you.' After a relationship is established, respectful nick names can be welcomed and endearing.

158. **Do not go out expecting to ride on your player's dime.** Never take advantage of your player by assuming he's fine covering the bill. Your broke mentality will be a self-fulling prophecy as long as you continue to take advantage.

159. **Do not say, "I'll catch you next time," and forget what you said.** Integrity is to remember your word and keep it. To assume others have forgotten how many times you've taken advantage of their generosity is to lose their respect. Game over.

160. **Do pick up the tab without hesitation if you see your player stressing out a little by hesitating or showing mental calculations.** Don't worry about equality, the universe has you covered.

161. **Do not try to gain a player's attention by connecting with their friend.** Games lose trust.

162. **Do not use jealousy to gain attention.** You'll only create confusion by sending mixed messages. Maintain your King by being pure with your intentions.

163. **Do show equal and respectful attention to a group of people.** Large parties will split off naturally. Remember, the person you're conversing with is your player, others are spectators until the board (conversation) switches. Do not discount the importance of the spectator. You could easily lose your King with them if they witness you make a dishonorable move.

164. **Do not rush to introduce yourself, bulldozing a prospective player.** You'll only push love away. Be patient, wait, observe, smile, make eye contact and approach casually. Open with a question. One move. Introduce yourself by keeping the conversation light and relevant to the venue. Then, let your player lead. If they don't pick

up on your lead, they're probably not interested. Bow out of the conversation gracefully.

165. **Do not approach your player by asking direct questions, as if interviewing from a résumé.** Direct questioning can be received as intrusive, giving the impression that you lack boundaries. To the discerning, this behavior is an immediate loss of your King because you've shown you can't be trusted to behave respectfully. Be humble and accept what your player chooses to disclose. Follow their lead, they'll tell you what they are comfortable sharing.

166. **Do pay close attention to your player's curiosities.** If your player has nothing to talk about, beware. His lack of interests indicates his lack of interest in himself. With no interest in himself, there's been little investment in personal growth. No investment indicates no self-worth. With no self-worth, there are insecurities. Insecurities lead to assumptions, defense, and accusations. Your player operates by the rules, not virtue. Pain is inevitable.

167. **Do recognize your player.** The player who is high maintenance, shows low energy, is overeager, too polite, boisterous, or uncomfortably stiff in demeanor, wears a veil to cover their inner reality—lacking self-worth, self-love, confidence, and self-esteem; all guarantee the loss of a King with the absence of virtue.

168. **Do not complain about a meal when it's on someone else's dime.** Whether or not the food is good, your player is still paying. Don't put them in a position where there's no remedy. Be respectable. The enjoyment of the food is secondary to the enjoyment of the company. Put your attention on your player.

169. **Do not defend a lie.** When you lie, you sacrifice your King whether or not you're caught by your player. The universe will bring your deception to light. To defend yourself is further work of the devil. To hurt your player, then defend yourself, adds insult to injury. Your

consequence is inevitable. Maintain your integrity. There is never a reason to lie.

170. **Do not be loud, obnoxious or boisterous.** Such a demand for attention is an imposition, signaling to your player to walk away. Any obvious need for attention is an embarrassment to your player.

171. **Do not talk to your player about people he doesn't know.** Your information serves as gossip and tells him you're not to be trusted.

172. **Do not ask your player superficial questions that serve your self-interest curiosity.** Actions will tell you everything. Asking without relevance is disrespectful. Allow your player to share naturally. Allow yourself the magic of recognizing your player.

173. **Do remember the pieces (virtues) relevant to the board.** You may not possess all of them, but awareness is key to gaining another. Think before you move.

174. **Do not waste time pondering assumptions as you try to fill in unknown facts to manufacture a conclusion.** Question yourself. Do you have all the facts? If the answer is no, suspend your suspicions. Be patient. Wait for the facts to surface.

175. **Do not try to steal your players thunder.** If he has cause to celebrate, celebrate with him. Do not bring negative energy to his positive energy. If he's excited, be excited. Being the devil's advocate is contrary to love. Stay on your side of the board by letting your Queen lead the way. Have faith that God also has a plan for your player. Show your love by supporting their excitement. Your relationship is priority before the cause for celebration. If you find it difficult to be loving, you may need to reevaluate the value of the relationship. Your player may have lost your respect a long time ago.

176. **Do not be quick to correct your player's favorable assumption about you or others.** Just go with it. Favorable assumptions give you something to live up to. Let people love you without your rebuttal or denial of their claim. Acknowledge and Accept, receive graciously.

177. **Do not pursue a player without first considering their perspective of you.** Does she know how to recognize a virtuous character? If not, she hasn't worked on her own. Be a friend first, without an agenda.

178. **Do remember your goal is to attract your desire.** You must vibrate higher, lifting your energetic field to bring your desire closer. To raise your vibration to love, Love harder. Use your virtues in all you do. Keep Faith close to you.

179. **Do not confuse tolerance with an invitation to play.** Tolerance looks like a one-sided engagement. Pay attention to make sure you're not monopolizing the conversation. If you suspect your behavior is being tolerated by another, your move is to Acknowledge and Accept their lack of interest. Gracefully move away from the table. The reverse is to be aware when you're being tolerant of your player. Are you engaged? Is he monopolizing the conversation? If he fails to give you your turn, there's no respect. You can't trust that. Game Over.

180. **Do allow the conversation to flow easily and effortlessly, showing interest with each exchange one move at a time.**

181. **Do recognize when you're being invited to play The Game.** There's the approach, introduction, and agenda. Pay close attention to these first moves, as they will tell you a lot about your player.

182. **Do not ignore the invitation.** Be respectful and gracious. Say 'yes' with a smile. There's always time to say 'no.' Remember to be a friend first, even when your player has other intentions.

183. **Do not get offended by the ignorance or audacity of your player.** Pause to keep from defending yourself with hurtful words.

184. **Do Acknowledge and Accept intrusive questions with grace, whether it be about height, weight, hobbies, kids, age, money, etc.** These are all measures of comparison and compatibility. Your player may be assuming you are equally interested in the same type of relationship they are pursuing.

185. **Do ask why these questions are relevant.** "I don't understand the question?" Wait for the response before you take another turn. "I don't understand the question," acknowledges their inquiry while accepting responsibility for your prerogative to comply. If your player says, "I'm just curious, is that okay with you?" You can respond with, "I don't mind you asking the question, but I don't understand the relevance?" Don't be afraid to hold your player accountable to their entitlement of information. Your player's move is independent of your move. Although you want your move to be relevant to the question, you don't want your move to give the impression that your player has free access to your business. Take the opportunity to create a boundary, demonstrating your intelligence and self-respect.

186. **Do be honest and transparent when your player says something offensive.** It's okay to say, "That hurt." This move makes your player accountable to his next move without you being guilty of defending or breaking another rule.

187. **Do not hassle, yell, degrade, or embarrass anyone in public.** The dishonorable behavior will forfeit your King to your player and spectators.

188. **Do exhibit self-respect by being respectable.** When in doubt, keep your mouth shut.

189. **Do not become desperate when you need an answer.** There are many ways that God has his angels deliver your answer. If you haven't received your answer, it's because you don't need it yet. Be patient and keep your Queen on the board.

190. **Do have faith that the universe is always working in your favor.** It's the ego that slips back into fear of the unknown "what if's."

191. **Do not believe that money is the answer to your need or desire.** God works in abundance. Abundance opens up all types of possibilities you may not be considering.

192. **Do believe love never fails to bring your desire.** Love, virtuous behavior, always delivers. A loving behavior always wins, the trick is to figure out how to love your way through your next move.

193. **Do not betray.** It's an instant game over. You can't cheat the system. Your player need not know the truth about what you're doing; the moment you choose to misbehave, justice is served. Know that the game is over.

194. **Do proclaim who you are as a silent promise to God.** If you say you're a man of your word, nobody needs to hear you say it; just be it.

195. **Do let people assume your ignorance.** It's a power move.

196. **Do not feel compelled to defend your character against your player's opinion of you.** Have faith that the truth will come to light. It's much more gratifying to allow them to be mistaken. Not only do you maintain your King, but you also get to use your mercy and humility piece which furthers the strength of your character.

197. **Do not assume there's a natural difference in character based on gender.** Both genders are equally hurtful when provoked. A woman isn't naturally loving if she's never been taught how to love.

198. **Do not be needy.** Neediness is a byproduct of insecurity and low self-worth. When you are needy, you can be quick to "fall in love." Your heart is susceptible to the slightest interest. If you cling to anyone who is willing to cling to you, you risk a broken heart, leaving you to wonder if there is anyone worth trusting. When you love yourself first, you'll be skilled to identify a worthy player.

199. **Do not doubt yourself.**

    Self-doubt is a byproduct of not having a move. More specifically, not knowing the right move. When you over think, realize you don't know the truth of your circumstances. Self-doubt is a lack of discernment. A lack of discernment is ignorance in knowing the difference between a virtue and a rule, right and wrong, love and fear. When these behaviors are mixed together, it's easy to understand how self-doubt creeps into our relationships. You won't need to doubt yourself when you know the difference between your pieces and the rules.

200. **Do not be ruled by trust issues.** When you have trust issues, it's because you can't trust your discernment. If you want to be confident in your ability to recognize your player, you must first recognize the player within you.

201. **Do not give in to ambiguity.** When there's an ambiguous statement, follow with a clarifying question.

    "We're taking it slow." — "What do you mean by 'it?'"
    "It's not like that." — "Then how is it?"
    "That's not what I meant." — "What did you mean?"

202. **Do learn to apologize without excuse or blame.** Acknowledge and Accept what is, then apologize without the words 'if' or 'but.' "I'm sorry *I* made you feel that way. It wasn't my intention. Let me try again." Do not say, "I'm sorry *if* I hurt you" or "I'm sorry *if* your feelings were hurt." The apology fails to be accountable for the infraction. Love is hearing what your player is *trying* to convey, then accepting the need for an apology.

203. **Do not break loyalty.** When your player confides in you, remember it's for your ears only. Keep your King on the board by holding yourself accountable to the heart entrusted to you. Appreciate and recognize the trust that's been given to you.

204. **Do not use confidential information as a weapon to retaliate against your player when your feelings are hurt.** Retaliation is a blatant betrayal contrary to love. Hurt feelings are often the result of misunderstandings. Pause and consider the assumptions.

205. **Do not make excuses or blame circumstances for your misbehavior.** Any rules broken will lower your vibration from powerful to weak, removing your supernatural protection, making you susceptible to the chaos created by the ego.

206. **Do exercise the pause to give yourself the opportunity to consider your feelings and each player's perspective before responding.** Imagine the King standing firm on his square. Allow time for patience and faith to guide you before acknowledging and accepting with grace.

207. **Do not give an underhanded compliment.** Self-awareness is knowing how to give a compliment without detracting, disqualifying, or comparing to others. I stress the pause. Think before you speak. "Oh, your salsa is delicious. My mom made the best salsa." The first move is a compliment. The second statement disqualifies the first, which is unnecessary and hurtful. There's no reason to discount your player's salsa by sharing a memory of your mother's salsa. Keep that part to yourself. Instead, show interest. Ask your player how he makes his salsa. Then, follow with an affirmative, "It's delicious." Stay present by speaking only of your player's salsa and not a memory of a different salsa. Love the one you're with.

208. **Do practice giving kind words without using the word 'but' to temper your player's ego.** How many times have you heard people say, "I think you're smart, but I don't want to give you a big head," or "You're great, but there are other great people too," or "I think you're beautiful, but I'm used to beautiful women." It's not necessary to temper your player's ego. It's more important for you to learn how to edify without fear of your player thinking they are better than you. Acknowledge your player. The easier it is for you to give credit to others, the more respect you'll earn. Edification builds a bond of appreciation and trust. The goal is to have lifelong relationships on purpose.

209. **Do not attempt to attract others with material things.** You'll only show others how materialistic and superficial you are. When you attract your player with material things, your player will be attracted to things rather than you. Be a person of substance. Focus on your virtues to increase your value.

210. **Do stay focused on your own business.** Your life should interest you more than the lives of others. You are the creator of your life. Know the difference between adding value to your life and giving your value to the lives of others.

211. **Do not feel the need or be compelled to fill the air with idle words of gossip, circumstance, or complaint.** These negative bouts of venting only serve as black smoke choking out an opportunity for love to grow. From the over flow of the heart, the mouth speaks. Listen to the way you order your words and how your player orders his words to express himself. Identify where the rules are being broken and if a virtue is present.

212. **Do not forget that life provides the test,** The Game provides the answer, and you're the player.

213. **Do be prepared to combine pieces you have available, but only one move at one time.** With your King on the board, wait. Be patient. Take a pause. Allow Faith to guide your move. Faith gives you the courage to use humor, compassion, and charity.

214. **Do not assume sexual overtones are welcome, invited or acceptable with your player.** This move should only be played within the confines of a consensual intimate relationship and no other.

215. **Do not tell your player to humble themselves.** This posturing demeans your player while also loses his respect. Stay in honor. Hold your tongue even when you're correct in your assessment. His arrogance is not your concern.

216. **Do not try to stop your player from cheating.** Be the watcher and wait for the dishonorable behavior. You must confirm with first-hand knowledge before calling game over.

217. **Do not subject yourself to accidental entrapment.** If you let the desire of the flesh cloud your good judgment, by default, your player will assume your consent to his character.

218. **Do not pretend to be humble while fishing for compliments.** Your player will see through your facade and recognize your insecurity. He will not trust you. Game over. Similarly, refrain from offering insincere compliments or flattery, in an attempt to create rapport with your player. Your vibration will be perceived as untrustworthy. Game over.

219. **Do be confident in your character as you work to eliminate the rules from your behavior and substitute your Virtues.** When you know who you are, others will to.

220. **Do not show affection to your player when he/she is disrespecting another player.** If you and your husband are with the kids, and he starts to belittle and demean their character in an attempt to control their behavior, do not side with him by way of an affirmative loving behavior. To interfere with his game with the child will lose your child's trust. Stay neutral. Keep your character separate.

221. **Do not confide in anyone about your best friend.** Your best friend is sacred. No Gossip. The betrayal will energetically destroy the relationship. If you want the relationship to continue, stay loyal.

222. **Do practice self-control, not control over your player, not in word, deed or behavior.** Self-disciplined gains favor. Self-control is the way to control your environment.

223. **Do not give your player an advanced warning on your next move, making premature promises assuming to know what move is coming.** You can only know your move after your player's move has come to pass.

224. **Do not ever tell a third party about your game with your player if the information will hurt the third party.** Stay in honor by keeping your games separate. The moment you hurt a player directly or indirectly, it's game over.

225. **Do not respond with arrogance, a self-inflated ego, condescension, patronizing, or sarcasm.** Never claim to know more than your player. Don't name drop, insult your player's intelligence, or dismiss your player's move.

226. **Do not fear a momentary sacrifice of your reputation.** Remain humble and withstand the injustice knowing everything hidden will come to light. Have faith.

227. **Do not chase your player.** You'll push love away. Attract your player with a loving vibration of care, safety, and trust. Show your interest by being a friend. Being a friend is first in all trustworthy relationships.

228. **Do not defend yourself when you've caused your player to walk away.** Acknowledge and Accept respectfully that you've lost your King. Execute diplomacy when the game is over. When your player makes a wrong move, you must have confirmation about the reason why your trust was lost before calling Game Over.

229. **Do not have expectations about anything other than a general anticipation of favor coming your way.** Expectations from your player lead to disappointment and accusations. Your disappointment and accusations position your player to defend and deny. It's a slippery slope causing the end. The dishonorable behavior will lose the relationship.

230. **Do recognize your expectations and question yourself before making a move.** "Why am I expecting this? Am I entitled? Why? Does my player have reason to know of my expectation?" Look at yourself from your player's side of the board.

231. **Do not confuse your spectator with your player.** Your player (a) is conversing with you. Spectators, whether it be your wife, friends, or circumstances, are not player (a) in front of you. If your player (a) speaks to your wife or your friends, the board switches. You are now the spectator. Don't interfere. Watch to see how they play their game.

232. **Do not feel the need to explain the reason for your move.** If your move is virtuous, your player will never question your motive. There's no need for you to explain.

233. **Do not be obstinate in your opinion or beliefs.** Be open to your player's beliefs and opinions in order to recognize your player's way of processing. Acknowledge and Accept his position. It's not necessary for you to convert him to your beliefs. It's more important for you to understand your player to correctly behave in Love (virtue).

234. **Do not be victim to substance abuse.** Game Over.

235. **Do learn to love.** How?

    Be the watcher. Keep the rules in mind and notice when you and others break the rules.

    Practice grace by knowing the rules. Grace is knowing what to say and when to say it. If you fail to have a loving and diplomatic response, stay quiet.

    Keep your side of the board clean. Let your player play without interference.

236. **Do not underestimate the power of the pause.** Take your time with your move. The pause allows you to think about your perspective and change your view to align with love. It also makes your player impatient because they're expecting you to respond immediately. When you don't, your player will often take another turn assuming you need help with your decision. The longer you pause, the more moves they make. Each of their moves will direct you on how to make one precise move.

    Example: She's making dinner—steak and asparagus. He walks in and says, "I had asparagus for lunch." She's upset because she feels unappreciated for her effort. He's feeling guilty for mentioning it and is now resentful for having to walk on eggshells. They appear to be fighting over asparagus, but in reality, they both had expectations. She expects him to say thank you and eat it, and he expects her not to take offense. Both end up being defensive.

The Move (a): She tells him her plan for dinner, giving him the opportunity to accept or reject. (b): She could make enough dinner for both of them to enjoy but save his portion if he chooses not to eat it. Her move predicates his. Conversely, he could have told her in advance what he ate for lunch, giving her the opportunity to change the dinner plan, or he could just eat the asparagus again for dinner. Their respect for each other takes precedence over their lack of communication about the meal.

237. **Do be mindful of your tone when texting.** For example, "Call me" is an order. Any *order* to do something is disrespectful, even when the intention is to be quick and concise. It's better to convey your message with respect to your player. Be loving in tone. "Baby I need to talk to you when you get a minute," or "Do you have a minute? I need to talk with you," or "I'm going to call you in five minutes, is that okay?" Show respect for your player; it will keep your game in play and earn you further respect.

238. **Do embrace the difference between responsibility and expectation.** Responsibility is what we hold for ourselves; expectation is what we hold for others. Let go of expectations. We can't hold others accountable for our standard of responsibility.

239. **Do not attempt to ease your player's pain during an argument by reminding them of yours.** This is a guilt move. Simply, acknowledge your player's pain, listening without judgment or taking offense. Watch for the virtues they are missing, the rules being broken, and the expectation they assume to be entitled. Do not correct your player. Just observe with compassion until it is your turn.

240. **Do practice empathy.** Empathy is the ability to feel what your player is feeling. When you are consoling, you may share a similar experience, but only to the extent of being relatable. Do not take this opportunity to turn the focus on yourself and your story.

241. **Do not settle for a player who has low standards because you're afraid of being alone.** Maintain your Queen by holding to your high standard of character. When you make allowances for the wrong person to fill the space, there's no room for the right one to step in.

242. **Do work on becoming the person you wish to find.** If you want affluence, you must learn how to make money. If you want influence, you must learn how to earn respect. If you want honor, you must work on becoming virtuous. If you want to find someone with impeccable character, understand the definition of character and become it. Opposites may attract, but a good character will only commit to the same good character for the long haul.

243. **Do not attempt to gain love or approval by serving your player.** To serve first without earning your players respect will lead the way for entitlement. Conversely, when you demonstrate self-respect, your player will recognize your character as you serve. A King never bends over backward to serve his Queen or his Kingdom. He bows in service as a respectful gesture. If a man chases a woman around, bending over backward to please her, she will accept his offer and continue to take freely from him without reciprocation, gratitude, or respect. A King will maintain personal standards and virtuous behavior, to gain her respect. With respect, she will honor him—by submission when necessary.

244. **Do not make the mistake of thinking one virtue is enough to win the game.** You need all of the pieces. For example, to be humorous is a virtue, but it's only one piece. If you use the same virtue all the time, your player will know your one move. Your player will lose respect for your game.

245. **Do take the path of least resistance with focus on the destination.** A river flows over the rocks and around the dam easily and effortlessly to the sea. Be ready to go with the flow of life instead of being stubborn in the course of your direction. Everything happens for your good when you're being true to your heart. Just go with it.

246. **Do understand what a proclamation is and how to be accountable to it.** To proclaim is a promise to yourself. To be accountable is to show your player the integrity of your proclamation. Failure to be accountable is to change your mind, idea, or plan about your proclamation without giving notice, or failing to remember the original thought, promise or plan given to your player. Don't make promises. Without accountability, you lose integrity. Game over.

247. **Do not confuse what you want to hear, (for example, "I love you") with what your player wants to say.** Meaning, your player may already know what you're wanting to hear, but he is purposely avoiding it. Acknowledge and Accept without pressure or coercion.

248. **Do not over promise and under deliver.** It's best not to say anything and just deliver. Create opportunities to deliver beyond your immediate family and friends. Love harder.

249. **Do not concern yourself with competition.** There is no competition with others, only with yourself to attain self-mastery. God wants to express through you. Focus on being an expression of love.

250. **Do listen to Rife frequencies, binaural beats, and singing bowls for cellular cleansing.** You have many resources to help you elevate your vibration. Use them.

251. **Do utilize intermittent fasting for good health and weight management.** Sixteen hours without food helps the body to repair, use stored energy, and facilitate a deeper meditation. Keep your body feeling good. If your body doesn't feel good, you'll be less motivated to stay accountable to virtuous behavior.

252. **Do remember the power and importance of a kiss.** This may appear to be obvious, but the timing and application is important. Never impose a physical gesture on your player without invitation or consent. Bad timing loses respect for both players.

253. **Do remember that it's better to love than to be right.** No matter how wrong or off base your player's perception is, never argue to be right. If the relationship is important, concede by listening and acknowledging their view point. You don't have to agree, nor should you "agree to disagree." That statement is contrary to love. Aim to understand your player. You'll have your turn to clarify if the subject matters. In the heat of the moment, lay down your sword and hear them out. This is especially important when you know your player is not going to budge on their position. Keep the peace and your honor by using your ears and not your mouth.

254. **Do not ever try to hide your ill intention, habit, or addiction from your player.** If you're not proud of what you're doing, don't do it.

255. **Do be clever and coy when planning a nice surprise for your player.** If you want success, do not allude to the surprise or you will risk disappointment by creating expectations. The anticipation of the surprise may be more than the surprise itself, or your surprise may not be received according to your expectation. In either case, promises and expectations are rules not to be broken.

256. **Do not confuse transparency with dishonesty.** Transparency is being truthful with relevant information. Offer only what is relevant to the inquiry. Withholding irrelevant information is not being dishonest, it's a skillset of concise communication. You're not being dishonest when there's no reason to be transparent. Dishonesty is to withhold relevant information that would change your players perspective.

257. **Do not impose your standards onto your player. Standards are personal values for one's own behavior.** You can only like or dislike your player's standards, values, and behavior and be accountable to your own. You may like your bed made and your player likes his car clean. These are *personal preferences*, but if you both believe in keeping your word, then you share the same virtue; integrity.

258. **Do remember diversity is presented in nature—just as it is in humans.** Trees, flowers, and animals come in all shapes, sizes and colors. We are no different. All variations contribute to the beautiful landscape. To divide and mark as superior based on color, shape and origin is to demean our Creator. All of life is a manifestation from the one source, the seed of love. Respect the creativity of the artist.

259. **Do remember Patience.** If you don't have the answer when you believe you need it, be patient, have faith, and stop worrying about the unknown future. Relax. The universe knows what you need and will provide when you need it. If you don't have it, it's because you don't need it. Trust God's plan for you. You're not alone.

260. **Do not be misled by those who recite wise quotes and passages.** Quotes fail to prove good character. Pay attention to behavior.

261. **Do not *expect* your player to remember positive things you've said or done in the past.** His behavior toward you will provide evidence of respect.

262. **Do not *substitute* your apology with a gift.**

263. **Do not blame others for your decisions. Blame exposes your insecurity.** A simple example is to substitute eggs in your cake recipe. You realize that your cake is less than delicious. Later, you cover your mistake by blaming John for not buying eggs. If someone notices that the cake tastes different, simply tell them you didn't have eggs. Don't put John in a position to defend himself.

264. **Do not make excuses or allowances for your player when you realize he doesn't have all his pieces (virtues) on the board.** If you become attached to your player and decide to ignore his behavior, you're setting yourself up for heartbreak. Don't be foolish to believe your player will change and become more virtuous over time. Your tolerance will only perpetuate his behavior. Believe who he is when he sits at the table. He will either promote a lifelong relationship daily, or he will lose your trust and cause the game to be over. The more apt you

are at separating the pieces from the rules, the more confident you'll become in your decision to stay or leave the table. When you recognize that your player doesn't have patience, be confident; what you see are control issues. His faith is off the board. Losing his King is inevitable. Watch closely as he continues to break more rules. Ask yourself if you trust this player. If the answer is no, it's time to move on.

265. **Do not be fooled by a player giving you advice or attempting to portray "being on your side."** The agenda of most players, whether conscious or unconscious, is self-serving. Self-interest is always in play until you and your player master The Game. Keep the rules close to you.

266. **Do not retaliate when your player *makes a hurtful move*.** Pause. Protect your King. Be the watcher. First consider your perception and expectations to make sure you're not making assumptions. There may be a misunderstanding. Be patient.

267. **Do not *look* for affirmation or confirmation from your player.** Your player will assume he's been invited to tell you how to play your game. Your insecurity gives him the liberty to remove the boundary and start telling you what to do. Be mindful of your insecurities or you'll lose the respect of your player. He'll start to act like you're not capable of making your own decisions.

268. **Do not assume to understand your player before he makes his point (move).** Be careful not to prematurely agree before listening, then interrupt his speech with your spin on his point. You could be wrong about your presumptions. Love listens patiently. Make sure that what he is saying is heard without interruption so that you may respond appropriately. Otherwise, you run the risk of pushing love away by drawing your own conclusions. Conversely, watch how your player interrupts you with their defense. Don't insist on being understood when he doesn't care to understand. Recognize his lack of respect. It will help you with your discernment later. When you seek to understand you ask questions.

269. **Do not expose your insecurities by sharing all of your weaknesses with your player.** Remember, the opportunist is looking for your trust. If your player is your partner, he will change from sympathetic to controlling when given the right circumstance. Be mindful of your personal weaknesses: spiritual, financial, and emotional.

270. **Do not use poverty to pull on your friends' heart strings.** This dishonorable move will lose your players' respect for you. Know your financial situation and make decisions based on your ability to contribute. Do not make excuses. Your money is your business. Not public knowledge.

271. **Do not assume that your player wants or needs a daily update on your circumstances.** You're not the nightly news. Wait for the inquiry. Use discernment before sharing unsolicited stories.

272. **Do not threaten to make a hurtful move.** Your threat will lose the trust of your player and cause an insecurity which manifests into a self-fulfilling prophecy. Game over.

273. **Do not allow money to come between you and your player.** The Game is about learning how to love, not how to control the money. You can't serve both.

274. **Do not beg your player to return to the board after you've lost the game.** Have dignity by accepting the loss without disrespecting yourself or your player. Once your King is lost, any attempt to play other pieces (humor, forgiveness, grace, etc.) to salvage the relationship will be in vain. If your player does return, know that your King is off the board. Your player doesn't trust you. The end is inevitable. Self-love is evidence of self-respect. When it's time to leave the table, do it without demeaning yourself or your player. The rules still apply even when it's game over.

275. **Do not make an out-of-turn move when your player fails to make a move according to your expectations.** Be patient. Wait for his move, then take the time you need to respond with virtue. Do not be

tempted to persuade your player to make a move for your benefit. Let your player play his game. Keep quiet while he makes his decisions. Do not interfere regardless of your temptation for personal gain. Each move must be of free will for each in order to accurately recognize your player.

276. **Do not distract your player's pain with a consolation prize if your player is hurt or disappointed with another player from a different game.** If the pain doesn't involve you, apologize for the misconduct of the other player, but be careful not to assume responsibility for the move.

"You know I'd never lie to you, right?" Or "You still have me, right?" This creates confusion with your player as you direct attention to yourself. Remember to acknowledge your player's pain with compassion. Sit in silence, hold them, and simply say, "I'm sorry." Your loving energy will transfer to your player. Once they feel better, you're ready to get a bite to eat, play, and joke around.

Although promises can offer a light of hope and happiness for the future, they are dangerous. Making promises shines a light on your integrity, creating an expectation within your player. The move tests his patience until you deliver. Unfulfilled promises bring doubt, assumptions, and accusations when the expectation for delivery doesn't look promising.

277. **Do not struggle with resistance.** Resistance provides direction. There's no need to break through a resistance barrier. You have a 360 degree view of opportunity to find another way to arrive at your destination. Be flexible with your course. Follow the course that leans toward love. Imagine going down a river in a canoe. When you come to a fallen tree, don't bust through the barricade. Take the turn. Follow the direction of the current. Love is easy and effortless.

When your player is combative, argumentative, defensive, denies, or blames, he suffers from "I'm not good enough syndrome" or insecurity.

Your move is compassion. He needs love and reassurance. If your player is *easily offended,* he is probably suffering from a low sense of self-worth. Notice how he resorts to denial, confusion, circle talk, blame, and verbal insults to cover his pain. Pause. Accept his fight in silence. Recognize his character. He's not going to change as long *as you're in play.*

A player with a low sense of self-worth will sometimes mask his insecurity by being overly accommodating to establish his value. He will go to great lengths to be pleasing, but when he's called out on his dishonorable behavior, he will defend himself, claiming nothing is ever good enough.

Be careful when making more than one move without honoring your player's turn. It can very easily escalate to a downward spiral of breaking the rules. Multiple moves are caused by assumptions, followed by accusations, and finally defending the behavior. No amount of justification or excuses will help you maintain your King. Practice one move: Patience.

278. **Do not jump to conclusions based on fear-based assumptions.** Have patience. Wait for confirmation or an opportunity to ask your player a question. Always look for clarity before casting premature judgment.

279. **Do not be quick to correct the player who insults your intelligence.** It's better to let him underestimate you. This gives you the advantage of recognizing his character further. Consider the insult carefully to be sure you're not the one getting offended unnecessarily. Similarly, do not allow yourself to get caught up in your player's gossip about another. Soon, he will say the same about you. A gossiper is not to be trusted.

It will benefit you to keep in mind that there is more than one way to solve a dilemma. If you feel like you're spinning your wheels, it's not the right path. When the path is correct, it comes together easily and effortlessly. When you feel defeated, let go and have faith. The universe will bring an answer.

Once you identify your player's method of operation—whether it be as a bully, through low self-worth, selfishness, being unforgiving, demanding, or controlling—you must accept who he is without making excuses. See it and accept it. You can't change your player. Imagine a snake. You recognize that a snake will bite and rattle his tail; that's his nature. Don't try to negotiate with the snake thinking he will agree not to bite. He will, it's his nature. Never assume a snake will transform into a loyal dog. Recognize the serpent and walk away.

280. **Don't try to solve your player's riddle of circumstances.** The drama bag is only looking to share what's in his bag. Your player is not looking for a solution. Disregard the details. Watch for rules and pieces.

281. **Do not make racial comments in jest.** Your player will recognize your lack of boundary. The move is dishonorable and will result in the loss of your King.

282. **Do not assume it's your players responsibility to help you improve your game.** Only you are responsible for your own words and actions. If your player attempts to correct your game by exposing the truth to you about yourself, accept it as an act of love no matter how poor the delivery.

Part 11

POINTS TO REMEMBER

- **Wherever you go, there you are.** No amount of distance or travel will solve the pain from unresolved issues. Although a change of scenery is good for the soul, it's not the remedy for the underlying problems caused by the destruction of your choices.

- **Face your fears,** walk through the fire. The beauty of the fire is that there will be a gift waiting on the other side, a reward for your courage. If you try to resist, avoid, or suppress the challenge, the fire will continue to get closer until you get burned. Walk through it or face the challenge again.

- **Lower vibrational beings will expect you to come down from the castle to defend yourself against their challenge.** Don't do it. Take into account the elevation of your player's standards. Do not divulge personal information to a player with a lower standard of behavior than yours. Be discreet with private business or else expose yourself to the retaliation of judgment, ridicule, and betrayal.

- **A man who works hard to build his character will never succumb to the flesh of an average woman.** Only a Queen with equal character will be worthy of his affection. Her respect for him will be met with his complete devotion.

- **You have all that you need to give all that you have today.** Don't make excuses and promises for tomorrow. Whatever you have today is enough. That's all that's required.

- **It's better to love than to be right.** Anyone can be correct with their facts, but the virtuous player will choose to love first. Being right is overrated as it loses friendships instead of gaining respect. It's intrinsically rewarding to be able to acknowledge and accept your player objectively. Even when you are correct, the process of proving it is delicate and requires grace. Ask questions. When in doubt, choose peace over conflict.

- **When a man looks for financial equality with a woman, he doesn't see himself as a leader.** A King does not value a woman by her money; he values the character she brings to his table. A King takes pleasure in providing for his Queen.

- **To be disagreeable is contrary to love.** Acknowledge and Accept. Consider the challenge objectively and offer a solution. Strive to be agreeable even when you disagree with your player. Be agreeable first by acknowledging and accepting what is being said before gracefully asking a question.

- **The status of Royalty (the Most High) must be earned.** Anyone who assumes a position of royalty but fails to behave honorably will be rejected by others.

- **When you are verbally attacked with accusations, ask questions.** Don't defend. Acknowledge and accept what your player is saying as well as what they are trying to say. For example, a woman accuses a man of thinking another woman is attractive. His natural response is to deny the accusation or dismiss her perception. Neither are loving responses. Is she breaking a rule by accusing? Don't defend yourself. Second, what is she not saying? She's inadvertently saying she's insecure about her own attractiveness. The correct move is for him to acknowledge and accept what she has exposed, add humor, and a compliment.

Something like, "I was thinking that woman was attractive, but something is missing. Oh yeah, she's just not you, baby!" Three virtues in one move—

acknowledge and accept, humor and grace. Remember, grace is knowing what to say and when to say it. Let's try another.

Your boss wants to talk with you. You're being accused of eating someone's sandwich from the lunch room. You didn't do it. The knee-jerk reaction is to deny and say you didn't do it with a follow up question as to why he thinks you ate it. This is an incorrect response 1) because you're defending yourself, and 2) because you're making two moves. The correct response is to acknowledge and accept with a question, then wait for a response. "I ate the sandwich?" Pause and wait for a response. Your player's next move will either expose the truth about his assumption or it will prompt him to confirm his accusation. You're in position to control the conversation with your virtues each time your boss makes a move before your next move.

- **When you break a rule, or disappoint your player, take responsibility without blame, excuse, or defense.** Apologize. Acknowledge and accept the result of your move whether intended or not. Do the right thing right now without making promises for the future. If you make an assumption, admit and retract as soon as you realize it.

- **You will not be justified by your player if you bully him.** It's never right to make someone feel bad in an attempt to bring your point home.

"I told you I was right. I don't know what makes you think you're smarter than me?"

"Did I tell you I was right? Maybe you should do your research before you talk to me." Each of these responses will sacrifice your King. Any move you make that prompts your player to think you're an asshole, is game over. Why? Because nobody trusts an asshole.

- **Self-awareness is acknowledging your need for love, joy, laughter, fulfillment, recognition, and money.** Acknowledge the same needs in your player. When you're able to provide these things for your player, you fill your own cup by serving others. Every day presents an opportunity to fulfill one of these needs for someone else every day. Keep your eye open for opportunities to be kind.

- **When you have to play with someone who does not like you, observe to see if the problem is with you or with your player.** Your player could be struggling with an insecurity and be mirroring the problem in you. Put your assumptions and defenses down. Acknowledge and accept your player's dislike, then be kind and attentive when your player is at your table.

- **If you want to be adored, work on being adorable.** The characteristic of being adorable is to have a childlike innocence and humility. Being adorable is extremely attractive, bringing further opportunities.

- **Never use scripture during an argument to support your position.** Any self-righteous approach will create distance dividing you and your player. Once there's a crack, the divide will only get bigger.

- **Once the game is lost, walk away.** Do not allow your player to keep pushing your buttons by repeatedly breaking the rules. Once you recognize their game (betrayal, cheating, lying, accusing, making excuses, and blaming), do not make allowances with the expectation for change. The Game is over. To keep playing without a King on the board is a waste of your time. To continue to play after respect is lost is attachment. Attachment is dependency, not love.

- **When you are tempted to keep playing after The Game is lost, think of your player down in a hole in front of you.** You are watching them grab at your feet, trying to pull you in. Each time you allow yourself to be pulled back in, you get caught in their pain cycle. Don't let your ego fool you into believing you can pull them out. It takes strength of character to walk away from the dysfunction. Let them be responsible for their solution. Their poor moves are not your responsibility.

- **When texting or emailing, remember one move at a time.** Refrain from making multiple points and statements combined with questions. This too counts as more than one move and will open the door for miscommunication. Your words can easily be misconstrued. Avoid setting yourself up for having to over explain and clarify because your player is mixing and matching what you said according to his understanding. Make simple points and wait for a reply. The skilled player will consider the perception of the recipient and look for accusations and assumptions, before pushing send. Try to wait for a reply before sending another message to avoid conflict. Let the communication roll out concisely one response at a time by respecting your player.

- **When you see a way to achieve a goal, but it depletes your energy, pause to consider.** Too much effort combined with delayed gain is not the right direction. Spinning your wheels is a sign from the universe that you're not on the right path. When you make the right move, you'll feel instant gratification. If you don't, chances are you didn't pursue your goal with passion. Be persistent, but fluid, with your path to get there. Be willing to change course if necessary, while maintaining a clear vision of your destination. The goal is to feel good now. Love is easy and effortless.

- **Learn to ask questions.** Questions are your most valuable tool especially with accusations and assumptions. Assume nothing and don't defend.

- **Boredom, depression, or complacency is a lack of vision.** See your perfect life with your mind. Your vision is your 'why' and will create a natural sense of motivation.

- **When you find yourself in the company of disagreeable people—those who challenge your ideas, take over your sentences, feel they know more than you, hush your opinions, demean you, and negate your suggestions—be agreeable.** Let them talk, lead, and direct, acknowledging and accepting their arrogant superiority. A sunny disposition and willingness to learn will let down their guard. This is the route to your success. This marks a change in The Game as each small step builds his trust in you, enabling you to lead with love.

- **Discernment is knowing how to make incremental moves while being disrespected by your player.** When you are under a verbal attack, be patient, let him make all his points while you graciously acknowledge and accept (incremental move). This lets him know you're listening, until he is all talked out and the storm is over. When the fire goes out, walk away from the table. Nothing more needs to be said.

- **When your player is abusive, verbally, mentally, or physically, acknowledge and accept what you see, and remove yourself from the relationship.** Do not try to change him by reasoning, defending, or reminding your player about who you are. You will not change his character or his behavior. Move away in silence. Maintain self-respect (honor). "I hear you. I apologize. I won't bother you again."

- **Stay away from a debate.** A debate serves to divide you and your player and promotes the pursuit of being right instead of seeking to understand. It is better to acknowledge and accept your player's position asking questions than to insist on changing his mind.

- **Stay away from using the words 'always' and 'never.'** These two statements are absolute, without allowance, which automatically sets you up for failure.

Part 12

THE WORD

For many, the Holy Bible is the foundation for all knowledge and wisdom. It's a curious and timeless book of stories, laws, instruction, history, parables, and lessons to help us understand how best to navigate our life experience. The esoteric teachings can be vague and confusing if you don't know how to read and receive the message. If you desire a true understanding according to our purpose, it's best to be humble and ask the Holy Spirit for understanding. When you ask God for understanding, you're given a higher level of consciousness that the ego is incapable of reaching. Don't be afraid of or shy away from the Bible's teaching. Soon, the words will speak to you in a way that only your heart can understand. Know that every effort you make to become one with love will be supported by the universe. Your faith will increase exponentially.

It's been my experience, that each time I open my Bible I'm given an answer or confirmation more complex than my previous understanding. I cannot stress the brilliance within its pages. And although the Bible was written for the collective, its message speaks directly to the spirit of the individual. Your experience with God is very distinctive as love manifests itself through your physical existence. The more you let go of your ego (devil), the more you allow the spirit of your true self to expand in ways you never thought possible. For this reason, be cautious before looking to another man for "religious" interpretation; your ego is at risk for being led by another ego. Instead, surrender to the rules and virtues in order to let the Spirit guide you in truth. Just as you wouldn't go to your neighbor to understand your spouse, don't go to another man to understand your relationship with God. Love must be intimate and direct.

When reading the following scripture, remember that God is love. Love is virtuous. When you separate the rules (Satan) from the pieces (Love) you are able to align your behavior with the Most High vibration. It is imperative that you reflect upon your mental view of what God is to be clear in your comprehension. If you read scripture with a mental picture that God is separate from you, you will sacrifice your true power by separating yourself from what you truly are—love. By default, your separation empowers the opposing force in you—your ego. To master The Game, you must become one with love. God is your best friend, and you represent. His breath lives in you. You are both the steward and manifest of the greatest force in the universe.

The wisdom of the Bible is the foundation for The Game. My notes are not meant to impose a specific interpretation of scripture, but rather, they are meant to help you understand how the rules and pieces are synonymous with the messages in the Word. Always refer to your higher power to gain a greater understanding.

$Part$ 13

TO KNOW LOVE IS TO KNOW GOD

"For I know the plans I have for you, says the Lord."

Jeremiah 29:11

Love has a plan for you. When you love, the plan for your life
becomes visible to you; your direction becomes clear.

*"For I will give you the words and wisdom that
none of your adversaries will be able to resist or contradict."*

Luke 21:15

Love will give you the words.
Grace is knowing what to say and when to say it.

"Enter the narrow gate."

Matthew 7:13

In a world filled with negative influence, propaganda, lies, fear, and the
struggle for money, entering the narrow gate is to love, and to love only.

*"Not everyone who says to me 'Lord, Lord,'
will enter the kingdom of heaven, but only he
who does the will of my Father who is in heaven."*

Matthew 7:21

Praying is not the key to the kingdom. Doing is the key.
It's not enough to proclaim to know God, to believe in God,
or to pray to God. To enter the kingdom, take action to
become one with God.

*"Therefore, everyone who hears these words of mine
and puts them into practice is like a wise man
who built his house on the rock."*

Matthew 7:24

A solid character builds a solid foundation.

"It will be done just as you believe it would be."

Matthew 8:13

It's to your benefit to believe only in good.

*"My message and my preaching were not with wise and
persuasive words, but with a demonstration of the Spirit's power,
so that your faith might not rest on men's wisdom,
but on God's power."*

1 Corinthians 2:4

The power of God is love in power.

***"No eye has seen, no ear has heard, no mind has conceived
what God has prepared for those who love him."***

1 Corinthians 2:9

Love yourself first. Prepare to be amazed.

"No one knows the thoughts of God except the Spirit of God."

1 Corinthians 2:10

The Spirit of God lives in you. It's your thoughts.

"Therefore, judge nothing before the appointed time."

1 Corinthians 4:5

Stop worrying. Stay present. One Move at a Time.

***"Don't you know that you yourselves are God's temple
and that God's Spirit lives in you?"***

1 Corinthians 3:16

Your body is the condition, that holds unconditional love.

"All things are yours."

1 Corinthians 3:21

Acknowledge and accept that everything in existence is yours right now.
The barrier is your perception of division. All is one.

*"Do everything without complaining or arguing
so that you may become blameless and pure children of God
without fault in a crooked and depraved generation."*

Philippians 2:14

"Pure children of God" strive to be blameless of breaking the rules.

*"Be wise in the way you act toward outsiders, make the most
of every opportunity, let your conversation be always full of grace,
seasoned with salt so that you may know how to answer everyone."*

Colossians 4:5

Listen to your player carefully so that you know what virtue to use
and when to use it.

*"Finally, brothers, whatever is true, whatever is noble,
whatever is right, whatever is pure, whatever is lovely,
whatever is admirable, if anything is excellent or praise worthy,
think about such things. Whatever you have learned or received
or heard from me, or seen in me, put it into practice
and the God of peace will be with you."*

Philippians 4:8-9

Live within your virtues. Everything good lies there.

"Therefore, prepare your minds for action; be self-controlled;
set your hope fully on the grace to be given you
when the Messiah is revealed.
As obedient children do not conform to the evil desires
you had when you lied in ignorance.
But just as he who called you is holy, so be holy in all you do;
for it is written: Be holy, because I am holy."

1 Peter 1:15 –16

You are no longer ignorant. Be obedient to love only.

"Whoever does not love does not know God, because God is love."

1 John 4:8

To love is to master your pieces without breaking the rules.

"My food is to do the will of him who sent me
and to accomplish his work."

John 4:34

Live to love. Let your expression be the hand of God.

"Again, truly I tell you that if two of you on earth agree
about anything they ask for, it will be done for them
by my Father in heaven."

Matthew 18:19

Seek to be agreeable.

*"Blessed is the man who does not walk
in the counsel of the wicked."*

Psalm 1:1

Wicked is a rule breaker.

*"Then the Lord God made a woman from the rib he had
taken out of the man, and he brought her to the man.
This is now bone of my bones and flesh of my flesh;
she shall be called 'woman' for she was taken out of man."*

Genesis 2:22– 23

Man came first to lead her with love.

*"All the ways of the Lord are loving and faithful toward
those who keep the demands of his covenant."*

Psalm 25:10

"Toward those" indicates there are others. Some live by virtue,
others by the rules.

*"My eyes are ever on the Lord for only he
will release my feet from snare."*

Psalm 25:15

Keep your eyes focused on love and you will protected.

*"Test me, Lord and try me, examine my heart and my mind;
for your love is ever before me and I walk continually in your truth."*

Psalm 26:2

Life provides the test; your virtues keep you committed in truth.

"Then you will come to call upon me and come and pray to me and I will listen to you."

Jeremiah 29:12

The Holy Spirit in you listens. Speak affirmatively.

"You will seek me and find me when you seek me with all your heart, I will be found by you declares the Lord."

Psalm 29:13

Seek to be virtuous and you will find God.

"Do not answer a fool according to his folly or you will be like him yourself."

Proverbs 26:4

Do not break the rules when your player is breaking the rules.

"As water reflects a face so a man's heart reflects a man."

Proverbs 27:19

Seek to reflect an honorable character

"Let another praise you and not your own mouth, someone else not your own lips."

Proverbs 27:2

No boasting. If you have to tell your player what you are, you're not that.

"Without wood a fire goes out, and without gossip,
contention dies down."

Proverbs 26:20

Hold your tongue and change your focus.

"Moreover, no man knows when his hour will come."

Ecclesiastes 9:12

To worry is futile. All you need is your next move.

"Come follow me, Messiah said,
and I will make you fishers of men."

Matthew 4:19

To follow is to do as I do.

"Love is patient, love is kind. It does not envy,
it does not boast, it is not proud."

1 Corinthians 13:4

Love does not cause pain.

"He fills my life with good things
so that I stay young and strong like an eagle."

Psalm 103:5

Love provides favor.

"A friend loves at all times."

Proverbs 17:17

Choose your virtues "at all times"

"Blessed are the pure of heart for they will see God."

Matthew 5:8

The pure of heart sees only good.

"With God all things are possible."

Matthew 19:26

With love all things are possible.

"Trust in the lord with all your heart and lean not on your own understanding. In all your ways acknowledge him and he shall direct thy paths."

Proverbs 3:5–6

Trust that virtue will direct your path. Don't rationalize the rules.

"Ask and it will be given to you, seek and you shall find, knock and it will be opened to you."

Matthew 7:7

Ask for direction. Seek understanding. Knock on the door to your desire.

"For the word of God is alive and active.
Sharper than any double-edged sword, it penetrates
even to dividing soul and spirit, joints, and marrow;
it judges the thoughts and attitudes of the heart."
Hebrews 4:12

The Game is always in play, you can't escape.

"When you sit to dine with the ruler, note well
what is before you, and put a knife to your throat
if you are a man given to gluttony. Do not crave
his delicacies for that food is deceptive."
Proverbs 23:1

Gluttony of the material world leads to unloving behaviors.

"Put on the whole armor of God, so that you can take your stand
against the devil's schemes."
Ephesians 6:11-16

The whole armor of God is knowing how to love using all of your virtues.
No harm will come to you.

"For the Lord gives wisdom; from his mouth come
knowledge and understanding."
Proverbs 2:6

Love provides wisdom. Speak with virtue, the result is knowledge
and understanding.

"Do not speak to a fool
for he will scorn the wisdom of your words."
Proverbs 23:9

Do not impose your wisdom of the The Game to a fool.

"If you say the Lord is my refuge, and make the Most High
your dwelling, no harm will overtake you,
no disaster will come near your tent. For he will command
his angels concerning you to guard you in all your ways;
they will lift you up in their hands,
so that you will not strike your foot against a stone.
You will tread on the lion and the cobra;
you will trample the great lion and the serpent.
Because he loves me, says the Lord, I will rescue him;
I will protect him, for he acknowledges my name."
Psalms 91:9-14

The Promise of protection will be delivered. You can put your fears to rest when you know you've committed yourself to making love your refuge.

"Wisdom will save you from the ways of wicked men,
from men whose words are perverse."
Proverbs 2:12

Wisdom is to know love. Perverse words break the rules.

"The fear of the Lord is the beginning of knowledge,
but fools despise wisdom and instruction."
Proverbs 1:7

Only a fool would discredit the instruction to Love.

"Listen, my son, to your father's instruction and
do not forsake your mother's teaching for they will be
a garland to grace your head and a chain to adorn your neck."

Proverbs 1:8-9

Pay attention to the instruction to love and look to nature.
Your results will make you proud.

"These men lie in wait for their own blood;
they ambush only themselves! Such are the paths of all who go
after ill-gotten gain; it takes away the lives of those who get it."

Proverbs 1:18-19

Cheaters never prosper.

"If you had responded to my rebuke I would have
poured my heart to you and make my thoughts known to you,
but since you rejected me when I called and
no one gave heed when I stretched out my hand,
since you ignored all my advice and would not accept my rebuke,
I in turn will laugh at your disaster."

Proverbs 1:23-26

Rebuke is the consequences of our actions
contrary to love that bring disaster.

*"Since they hated knowledge and did not choose to fear the Lord,
since they would not accept my advice and spurned my rebuke,
they will eat the fruits of their ways and be filled with the fruit
of their schemes. For the waywardness of the simple will
kill them, and the complacency of fools will destroy them,
but whoever listens to me will live in safety
and be at ease without fear of harm."*

Proverbs 1:29-33

The ill ways of the material world will be destroyed,
but those who love will live in safety.

*"For the Lord gives wisdom and from his mouth comes knowl-
edge and understanding. He holds victory in store for the
upright, he is a shield to those whose walk is blameless,
for he guards the course of the just and protects the way
of his faithful ones."*

Proverbs 2:6-8

Love provides wisdom through the Word.
To speak with love brings knowledge and understanding.

*"Let love and faithfulness never leave you,
bind them around your neck,
write them on the tablet of your heart,
then you will win favor and a good name."*

Proverbs 3:3-4

Keep your King, Queen, and Virtues on the board, and keep them close.
The right move will bring you favor.

"Blessed is the man who finds wisdom, the man who gains understanding, for she is more profitable than silver and yields better returns than gold."

Proverbs 3:13-14

Wisdom is knowing what love is. Love is the most valuable commodity.

"Do not be yoked with nonbelievers for what do righteousness have in common?"

2 Corinthians 6:14

A non-believer is one who is not a player in The Game.

"Anyone who does not love does not know God because God is love."

1 John 4:8

Without being committed to virtue,
one will not experience the Knowing of God.

"But the fruit of the Spirit is love, joy, peace, kindness, goodness, faithfulness, gentleness, and self-control. Against such things there is no law."

Galatians 5:22-23

"Against such things there is no law." Karmic consequence.

"Masters, provide your slaves with what is right and fair because you know that you also have a master in heaven."

Colossians 4:1

All are equal. No one escapes the order to love.

*"Be wise in the way you act toward outsiders,
make the most out of every opportunity, let your conversation
be always full of Grace seasoned with salt so that
you may know how to answer everyone."*

Colossians 4:5

Make every move according to virtue.

"Ask and it will be given to you."

Matthew 7:7

Ask for guidance, clarity, patience, and to be a gift for the greater good.

*"So, in everything do unto others
what you would have them do unto you
for this sums up the law and the prophets."*

Matthew 7:12

Play only with your Virtues.

*"I tell you the truth unless you change and become like
little children, you will never enter the kingdom of heaven."*

Matthew 18:3

Children don't worry about tomorrow.
Children have Faith that everything will be provided.

"Gossip betrays a confidence,
but a trustworthy man keeps a secret."

Proverbs 11:13

Keep your king on the board.

"The way of the Lord is a refuge for the righteousness,
but it is the ruin of those who do evil."

Proverbs 11:29

Love provides protection, the rules cause ruin.

"Do you see a man wise in his own eyes?
There is more hope for a fool than for him."

Proverbs 26:12

Wise in your eyes is to rationalize and make allowances for the rules.

"Do not speak to a fool for he will
scorn the wisdom of your words."

Proverbs 23:9

Recognize when the Ego rejects The Game.

"A generous man will himself be blessed
for he shares his food with the poor."

Proverbs 22:9

Charity and contribution.

"Listen, my son, and be wise and
keep your heart on the right path."

Proverbs 23:19

The right path is virtuous.

"If you argue your case with the neighbor
don't betray another man's confidence, or he who hears it
may share yours and you may never lose your bad reputation."

Proverbs 25:9-10

Stay in Honor to maintain your King.

The 7 ABOMINATIONS (Proverbs 6:16-19)
Haughty eyes…No Judgment.
A lying tongue…No Betrayal.
Hands that shed innocent blood…No Abuse.
A heart that devises wicked schemes…No Manipulation.
Feet that are quick to rush into evil…No boundary.
A false witness that pours out lies…No Honor.
And a man who stirs up dissension among brothers…No Gossip.

"Seldom set foot in your neighbor's house,
too much of you and he will hate you."

Proverbs 25:17

Mind your own business.

"A man can receive only what is given him from heaven.
You yourself can testify that I said I am not the Christ
but am sent ahead of him. The bride belongs to the bridegroom.
The friend who attends the bridegroom waits and listens for him
and is full of joy when he hears the bridegroom's voice.
That joy is mine and it is now complete.
He must become greater; I must become less."

John 3:27-30

The Spirit within must become greater than the Ego in the world.

"And we know that in all things God works for the good of those
who love him who have been called according to his purpose."

Romans 8:28

God gives favor to those who have been called according to his purpose to love.

"I tell you the truth until heaven and earth disappear,
not the smallest letter not the least stroke of a pen,
will by any means escape from the Law
until everything is accomplished."

Matthew 5:18-20

Every move you make will be met with consequence or favor.
It will come to pass as nothing escapes the Law.

"I tell you the truth, anyone who will not receive
the kingdom of God like a little child will never enter it."

Mark 10:14-15

A child receives love unconditionally.

*"Above all else guard your heart
for everything you do flows from it."*

Proverbs 4:23

Play only your pieces for every good deed flows from them.

*"Love is patient, love is kind. It does not envy, it does not boast,
it is not proud. It is not rude, it is not self-seeking,
it is not easily angered, it keeps no record of wrongs.
Love does not delight in evil but rejoices with the truth."*

1 Corinthians 13:4-7

Discern the pieces from the rules.

*"Therefore, you Kings be wise, be warned you rulers of the
earth. Serve the Lord with fear and rejoice with trembling.
Kiss the son, lest he be angry, and you be destroyed in your way,
for his wrath can flare up in a moment.
Blessed are all who take refuge in him."*

Psalm 2:10-12

Seek refuge in [him] - love your virtues.

*"For the Lord watches over the way of the righ-
teous but the way of the wicked will perish."*

Psalm 1:6

Operate in virtue and you will be protected against enemies
formed against you.

Princess Merrilee of Solana

*"Therefore, my dear brothers, stand firm. Let nothing move you.
Always give yourselves fully to the work of the Lord,
because you know that your labor in the Lord is not in vain."*

1 Corinthians 15:58

Stand firm in virtue. Never have doubt in your results.

*"Like a city whose walls are broken down
is a man who lacks self-control."*

Proverbs 25:28

A man who lacks self-control breaks the rules.

*"Through patience a ruler can be persuaded,
and a gentle tongue can break a bone."*

Proverbs 25:15

Patience wins the game. A gentle tongue uses virtue to overcome adversity.

*"Better to live on the corner of the roof than to
share a house with a quarrelsome wife."*

Proverbs 25:24

Less is more. Do not self-sacrifice for material things.

*"He who gives to the poor lacks nothing,
but he who closes his eyes to them receives many curses."*

Proverbs 30:27

Charity & Contribution

"Evil men do not understand justice,
but those who seek the Lord understand it fully."

Proverbs 28:5

Those who live according to virtue understand the consequence delivered
to those who don't.

"And when you pray, do not keep on babbling like pagans
for they think they will be heard because of their many words.
Do not be like them for your Father knows what you need
before you ask him."

Matthew 6:7-8

The Holy Spirit resides in you. Be confident your heart is known. Be grateful.

"Enter through the narrow gate for wide is the gate
and broad is the road that leads to destruction,
and many enter through it. But small is the gate
and narrow is the road that leads to life
and only a few find it."

Matthew 7:13-14

The narrow road is using only your pieces.

"So I say Love by the spirit, and you will not gratify the desires
of the sinful nature, for the sinful nature desires what is
contrary to the spirit, and the spirit what is contrary
to the sinful nature."

Galatians 5:16

Love by the spirit is to be virtuous.
The sinful nature is the ego that break the rules.

*"Wisdom calls loud in the street, she raises her voice
in the public square at the end of the noisy streets;
she cries out in the gateways of the city, she makes her speech,
'How long will you simple ones love your simple ways? How long
will mocking delight in mocking and fools hate knowledge?"*

Proverbs 1:20-22

Pick a side, wise or foolish?

*"If you love me, you will obey what I command
and I will ask the Father and he will give you another counselor
to be with you forever the Spirit of truth."*

John 14:15-17

Obey the command to love and you will be guided forever in Truth.

*"All this I have spoken while still with you,
But the Counselor, the Holy Spirit whom the Father
will send in my name, will teach you of things
and it will remind you everything I have said to you."*

John 14:25-26

The Counselor, The Holy Spirit is information.

*"But the world must learn that I love the Father and that
I do exactly what my father has commanded me."*

John 14:31

The command was to love.

"I am the vine; you are the branches. If a man remains in me and I in him, he will bear much fruit."

John 15:5

You and God are one. Remain in love and you will be abundant.

"This is my command, Love each other."

John 15:17

One command is the key to the universe.

"My command is this, love each other as I have loved you."

John 15:12

The command is simple. Be good. The Messiah is blameless of all the rules.

*"I have given them the glory that you gave me,
that they may be one as we are one. I in them and you in me,
so that they may be brought to complete unity.
Then the world will know that you sent me where I am,
and to see my glory you have given me because
you loved me before the creation of the world."*

John 17: 22 – 23

The Messiah is love, the same as God is love. The Messiah taught us how to be
Love, One with God so that there would be no separation.

God is in me. I Am that I Am.

Part 14

WISE MEN

It is my belief that these words can only be divine inspiration from the Holy Spirit. The depth of their meaning becomes profound as you master The Game. With greater understanding, comes greater appreciation.

I do not separate people, as do the narrow-minded,
into Greeks and Barbarians. I am not interested in the origin or race
of citizens. I only distinguish them on the basis of their virtue.
For me each good foreigner is a Greek and each bad Greek
is worse than a barbarian.

~Alexander the Great

A belief may be comforting. Only through your own experience,
however, does it become liberating.

~Eckhart Tolle

Nothing in the world can take the place of persistence.
Talent will not; nothing is more common than
unsuccessful men with talent.
Genius will not; unrewarded genius is almost a proverb.
Education will not; the world is full of educated derelicts.
Persistence and determination are alone omnipotent.
The slogan "press on" has solved and always
will solve the problems of the human race.

~Calvin Coolidge

Man knows much more than he understands.

~Alfred Adler

If you can make a mistake, you can make anything.

~Marva Collins

All good things are cheap, all bad things are dear.

~HD Thoreau

Do, or do not do, there is no try.

~Yoda

All conceptions are limitations of the conceiver.

~Neville Goddard

People settle for a level of despair they can tolerate and call it happiness.

~Soren Kierkegaard

Great men never require experience.

~Benjamin Disraeli

Fools you are who say you like to learn from your mistakes.
I prefer to learn from others and avoid the cost of my own.

~Otto Von Bismark

Time is an illusion of the happenings of the
things which have already occurred.
~Albert Einstein

The price of excellence is discipline.
The cost of mediocrity is disappointment.

~William Arthur Ward

It's better to keep your mouth shut and look like a fool
than to speak and leave no doubt.

~Earl Nightingale

Imagination is more important than knowledge.
Knowledge is limited.
Imagination encircles the world.

~Albert Einstein

Everybody is a genius.
But if you judge a fish by its ability to climb a tree
it will live its whole life believing that it's stupid.

~Albert Einstein

Any intelligent fool can make things bigger and more complex.
It takes a touch of genius and a lot of courage
to move in the opposite direction.

~Albert Einstein

A man should look for what is and not for what he thinks should be.
~Albert Einstein

*Education is what remains after one has forgotten
what one has learned in school.*
~Albert Einstein

*There are only two ways to live your life.
One is as though nothing is a miracle.
The other is as though everything is a miracle.*
~Albert Einstein

*Every adversity, every failure, every heartbreak
carries with it the seed of an equal or greater advantage.*
~Napoleon Hill

If you do not conquer self, you will be conquered by self.
~Napoleon Hill

*Success is good at any age, but the sooner you find it,
the longer you can enjoy it.*
~Napoleon Hill

*Don't wait. The time will never be just right.
Start where you stand and work whatever tools
you may have at your command;
and better tools will be found as you go along.*
~Napoleon Hill

*Deliberately seek the company of people
who influence you to think and act on building the life you desire.*
~Napoleon Hill

*The man who does more than he is paid for will
sooner be paid more than he does.*

~Napoleon Hill

*The grateful mind is constantly fixated upon the best.
Therefore, it tends to become the best.
It takes form or character from the best and will receive the best.*

~Wallace D. Wattles

*The very best thing you can do for the world is to make
the most of yourself.*

~Wallace D. Wattles

He who fears not has plenty of time.

~Wallace D. Wattles

Leisure is the mother of philosophy.

~Thomas Hobbes

Adopt a piece of nature: her secret is patience.

~R.W. Emerson

*Bad times have a scientific value.
These are occasions a good learner would not miss.*

~RW Emerson

Nothing great was ever achieved without enthusiasm.

~RW Emerson

Always do when you're afraid to do.

~RW Emerson

*You are already that what you want to be and your refusal
to believe this is the only reason you do not see it.*

~Neville Goddard

Imagination and faith are the secrets of creation.

~Neville Goddard

*Your opinion of yourself is your most important viewpoint.
You are infinitely greater than you think you are.*

~Neville Goddard

*The ideal we serve and strive to attain could never be evolved
from us were it not potentially involved in our nature.*

~Neville Goddard

*Believing that imagining creates reality,
dare to imagine you are now what you would like to be.
Do that and you are turning the water into wine.*

~Neville Goddard

*The biggest mistake that you can make is to believe
that you are working for somebody else.*

~Earl Nightingale

*Whenever we're afraid, it's because we don't know enough.
If we understood enough, we would never be afraid.*

~Earl Nightingale

*A good deal of frustration and unhappiness could be avoided
if people would do what they know they should do.*

~Earl Nightingale

Don't concern yourself with the money.
Be of service: build, work, dream, create!
Do this and you'll find there is no limit to
the prosperity and abundance that will come to you.

~Earl Nightingale

The word goes out, but the message is lost.

~Corsican Proverb

Make my enemy strong, so that if defeated, I will not be ashamed.

~Native American Proverb

Desire is proof of the availability.

~Robert Collier

The first principle of success is desire.
Knowing what you want.
Desire is the planting of the seed.

~Robert Collier

Start where you are.
Distant fields always look greener, but opportunity lies right
where you are. Take advantage of every opportunity of service.

~Robert Collier

When we are no longer able to change the situation,
we are challenged to change ourselves.

~Viktor Frankel

Faced with the choice between changing one's mind and proving that
there is no need to do so, almost everyone gets busy on the proof.

~John Kenneth Galbraith

Change always comes bearing gifts.

~Price Pritchett

Never mind searching for who you are,
search for the person you aspire to be.

~Robert Brault

One may understand cosmos, but never the ego.
The self is more distant than any star.

~GK Chesterton

I like to think before I speak, so it took me a while.

~Sir Kenneth Wayne Ya'ger

Testamentary Executor for the State of Grace IHS

Those who lack perseverance start out with the best intentions,
but lose focus and eventually give up on their dreams.

~Founder of Forbes magazine BC Forbes

It's not what happens to you,
but how you react to it that matters.

~Epictetus

The greatest virtues are those that are most useful to other persons.

~Aristotle

If we treat people as they are,
we make them worse,
but if we treat them as they ought to be,
we help them become what they are capable of becoming.

~Johann Wolfgang Von Goethe

*There is no such thing as working on only one leader-
ship quality or attribute. When you improve one, you
will invariably be improving several others.*

~John H Zenger and Joseph Folkman

The real fault is to have faults and try not to mend them.

~Confucius

Questions invoke thought.
Thought induces deduction.
Deduction leads to answers, and answers reveal the truth.

~Sir Kenneth Wayne Ya'ger

Testamentary Executor for the State of Grace IHS

P_{art} *15*

YOU'VE COME THIS FAR

If you've read this far, I applaud you.

Now that you know The Game, I pray you are inspired to renew your sense of responsibility for your purpose. You are the change for the next generation. As a committed player, you will create a beautiful life and legacy for yourself and others.

Take the reins as the master of your destiny. Your experience is promised to be the most inspiring and deeply satisfying ride till the end. With each victory you'll immediately be motivated to experience another.

> *True knowledge stems not from the authority of others,*
> *nor from a blind allegiance to antiquated dogmas,*
> *but instead, is a highly personal experience—*
> *a light that is communicated only to the inner most privacy*
> *of the individual through the impartial channels*
> *of all knowledge and of all thought.*
>
> ~Rogeri Bacon

As Rogeri Bacon so accurately stated, "It's a highly personal experience." The Game—*your game*, will deliver the gift specifically for you.

Part 16

SIMPLE, BUT NOT EASY

Many believe themselves to be generally good people, being a good judge of themselves and a good judge of character. The next chapter shows how The Game teaches us to understand ourself and our player with precision.

P_{art} 17

DIVIDE AND CONQUER

Now that we've divided loving behavior from unloving behavior, we'll look closer to gain a deeper understanding of consciousness. Consciousness is an expansion of knowledge gained from an elevated view of the whole to create an awareness about the complexity of humanities' emotional intelligence.

Part 18

GOD VERSUS EGO

The mind is the devil's playground. The devil knows exactly what to say (self-talk) and what to do (circumstances) to keep you distracted, emotional, and reactive. The devil is in play when he has you drawing conclusions based on fear. It happens very quickly.

Your Free Will gives you the option to love or not to love. The devil makes allowances to rationalize poor behavior in order to serve his pleasure, where the Spirit has the courage to make difficult decisions that are rooted in moral character.

The importance of the lesson needs to be studied. Without a clear understanding of allowances and rationalizing, one may not fully grasp the importance of surrendering fear to live by faith only. If you continue to stand with one foot on either side, claiming to have faith but serving the world of fear, by default, you will not experience the promise.

Don't be foolish to think you've got this. The Game requires the highest level of self-awareness to stay on the narrow path. With your constant and careful attention to the rules and pieces, and a healthy dose of the pause, your alignment begins to come together. You only need to make one move at a time. You don't need to know everything, only the move in front of you. There's no need for calculations, manipulation, or predictions about your player's responses.

"Therefore, judge nothing before the appointed time;
wait until the Lord comes.
God will bring to light what is hidden in darkness.

1 Corinthians 4:5

Part 19

THE FIVE GATES

RECOGNIZING YOUR PLAYER

1) PHYSICAL BEAUTY

2) PERSONALITY

3) INTELLIGENCE:
   UNEDUCATED, EDUCATED, HIGHLY EDUCATED,
   SELF-EDUCATED, ENLIGHTENMENT

4) CHARACTER

5) SPIRITUALITY

Part 20

THE FIRST GATE

PHYSICAL BEAUTY

Would you agree that everything beautiful is captivating? For something to be captivating, it must have an inherent gravitational pull that demands attention and admiration. Artistic expression is captivating. Art is inherently beautiful, evidence of love manifest. Art is everywhere the eye can see, the ear can hear, and the mind can conceive. Love is the creator of all artistic express which is beautiful; lavish gardens, a symphony, the stroke of a paint brush, a city scape, and every thought manifest to existence. Love is the creator of our beautiful world. Love is a creative consciousness where beauty is inexhaustible. Never take beauty for granted. Beauty is not a blessing to be used for the benefit of gaining money, power, and title.

God is love, love is truth, and the truth is beautiful. Of all the beauty in the world, nothing is more beautiful than the human expression. Your body is the manifestation of love realized. Your body enables you to touch God. What could be more beautiful? For this reason, people gravitate toward one another. Our energy fields pull together to be one. There is an inherent gravitational pull that captivates our attention, which creates a desire to know each other. God's instruction to procreate and fill the earth explains our desire to have sex. Making love is an energetic call to create a miracle, another God vessel. Our union is our creator's way of multiplying perfection. How could anything created from love not be beautiful?

THE DEVIL'S PLAYGROUND

Unfortunately, beauty is consumed by the ego. All that is superficial is the devil's ideal playground. There's not an easier method of control used to manipulate your mind and control your emotions than the meaningless desires of the flesh. The ego, being so arrogant, will not hesitate to sell your soul to have the beauty you perceive in others. Watch how easily you make allowances based on first impressions. Physical beauty diverts your ability to discern good character because it's natural to ignore unloving behavior in order to have the object of your desire.'

When your player is easy on the eyes, you'll tend to make allowances for the discrepancies in his character, especially if your player fits the "look" that suits your ideal. In The Game, we learn to look beyond the physical beauty of the vessel to focus on the virtues of character. Be careful not to make allowances and excuses in attempt to find the exception to the rule, by trying to lean on "nobody's perfect." This is your ego talking.

Put these words to the test. Soon you'll be able to see how physical beauty is the easiest way to recognize the underlying insecurities in your player. These insecurities lead to dishonorable behavior, a lost King. A lost King will break your heart—this, you can count on. Do not get enamored by your player's appearance. When you see the rules being broken, watch more carefully for your confirmation. Don't judge, observe. You don't want to make assumptions. Remember, you are learning to recognize where love is and where love is not. Protect yourself. If you make allowances or excuses for bad behavior, the pain will be much deeper when the relationship comes to an end. And it will come to an end.

UNDERSTANDING THE VESSEL

And God said, "Be fruitful and increase in number and fill the earth." Genesis 9:1. Boy, did the devil take this and run with it. Love wants us to procreate, duplicate and proliferate. That instruction to increase in number comes with a natural desire to become one with each other. The method to which we procreate, duplicate, and proliferate is sex. Sex is the method to "make" love. Making love is our greatest creative power evidenced by the delivery of another. Love is what we are and what we create. It's no wonder that the world is fascinated with the desires of the flesh. The body is beautiful, touching is beautiful, and being together as one body of love to create another body of love is the most beautiful and magnificent power to lift us to the Most High vibration. It begins with a magnetic attraction and ends with an uncontrollable explosion of euphoric fulfillment. Making love is sacred. Who doesn't want this?

It's understandable why this ultimate power is coveted by the dark forces of evil. Evil being that which should not be. The opposite of what is. That beautiful God-given power within you, if not careful, will be seized and redirected into a cesspool of insatiable self-destruction. Your beautiful flesh vessel, containing the value of your Trust, will be used to serve a selfish world that honors money, power, and title. Only the devil, with all his self-righteous arrogance, will judge that which he did not create and use the holy creation for his own self-serving world of fear to promote unloving behavior. He will take over your rational mind, make excuses for poor behavior to suppress the power of self-love. He will distract you with money and a false sense of power. You, as God's creation is akin to sheep who have lost their way in a world where your flesh determines the value of exchange.

Is it any wonder why so many people are victim to underlying insecurities about themselves when the devil sets the standard for perfection? When you believe that your appearance is the measure of your value, you become judgmental of others in order to inflate your own self-worth. Because of this, your self-worth is predicated on your physical beauty compared to those in fashion, instead of your self-worth being measured by your intrinsic beauty of character. In a physical world, character is lost in the shadows. When God is non-existent, your value will always be uncertain, subject to the opinion of others. That's when competition becomes inescapable because the devil will never accept you the way you are. Competition, expectations, rank, status, uncertainty, and insecurity are the reasons why people behave in ways contrary to love without even realizing it. The flesh becomes a weapon for self-destruction.

IDENTIFIERS

When your player steps up to the table, the first thing you'll recognize is his physical appearance. The following descriptions may offend you, as it appears that I'm making assumptions without knowing the person. I can assure you, you don't need to know the person or their story to know when your player *does not have a relationship with God. Evidence by their lack of self-worth in their presentation.* Make no mistake, this player will hurt you. These descriptions are not meant to discriminate, alienate, or judge your player, they serve to help you identify where love is missing.

The first rule of law is to love yourself first. The following examples give evidence to the contrary. Your understanding will become multi-dimensional when the five identifying gates open to reveal the truth. The first gate focuses on outward appearances. Typically, when your player is unbalanced or exaggerated about the superficial, he's harboring insecurities that are creating emotional instability. When you recognize these examples in your player, instinctively, you will not trust him. He is without a King. He's not to be trusted. Be careful not to give your heart to another heart that is broken. The Game is about *becoming love*, don't get lost. When your player has lost your trust, the play is to be respectful and respectable. It's important to understand *when* you don't respect your player. When you do respect your player, you'll be loyal, edify, and look to him for guidance. When you do respect your player, it will be easy to humble yourself and submit to his authority.

The body is the vessel of love that creates, duplicates, and manifests another love vessel. *It's not to be judged.* It's to be accepted as art, originating from the creator. Just as the animals of the planet are accepted for their differences and nature's beauty is without fault, we too must embrace our differences, as a brush stroke from the hand of God. Therefore, when you see a combination of physical attributes that please you, acknowledge and accept the beauty, but know that the personality of the vessel is not to be confused with the character of your player. Look beyond the obvious First Gate to see through to the next gate in order to recognize the truth in your player.

The human body in its natural form before and without alteration is the authentic manifestation of love.

The following list represents *physical behaviors when the ego takes over*. Physical behaviors are insecurities of the ego, not of God. If you see these behaviors in your player, pause. Watch carefully as he proceeds to break the rules. Don't be tempted to correct what you see. Observation in silence is key.

If your player...

- believes she has high standards because she identifies with physically beautiful people.
- constantly fixing, fussing, and rearranging herself.
- demeans others for the way they look.
- does not respect personal space—a close talker.
- doesn't smile.
- expresses himself by mutilating his body.
- finds fault with her physical appearance.
- fishes for compliments.
- has a distorted view about body fat, weight, and muscle.
- has bad oral hygiene.
- has trouble with eye contact.
- hinges his identity on owning name brands and high-ticket items.
- is disgruntled by those who don't meet her physical expectations.
- is high maintenance.
- is lacking in personal hygiene.
- is looking for people who are checking them out.
- is not concerned with good health.
- is overly concerned with germs.
- is overly focused on her face or body parts.
- is overly manicured.

- is preoccupied with every mirror.

- isn't comfortable with touching.

- lacks self-awareness.

- lies about age, height or weight.

- looks for others to confirm his attractiveness.

- looks to others, idolizing their look.

- never cares about appropriate attire.

- over accessorizes.

- over dresses for every occasion.

- over use of cosmetics.

- over use or exaggerated physical enhancements.

- suffers from an eating disorder, drugs, alcohol, or an addictive habit.

- uses their vessel to get what they want.

- voices his opinion about physical short comings.

- wears overly provocative clothing to attract attention.

- won't go out unless fully dressed or made-up.

These behaviors are outward physical expressions of inward disfunction. They reveal the insecurities of not knowing love rather than the security of self-love. When you recognize these insecurities, you can be confident this player will struggle with boundaries, standards, and virtue. You will get hurt if you fail to acknowledge.

Part 21

THE SECOND GATE

PERSONALITY

Personality has such vast identifiers; it's no wonder people get lost in the infinite field of possibility when looking to find their perfect romantic partner. Personality is where most people get lost in their discernment, because personality appears to encompass the entirety of our being. Like the tangled links of many chains, the aspects of who we are and how we will behave are difficult to sort out. You want to trust your player, but you're confused by the combination of adjectives used to describe them. Every player is unique in their own way—which is why you readily accept who they are until something they do tips the scales to make you feel good or bad about them. Even then, the emotion is fleeting as you become complacent, accepting them for the way they are because nobody's perfect. The Ego takes pride in making allowances for your player as you tolerate the dysfunction. There's no pride in self-sacrifice. Be careful, each time you make allowances for your player's dysfunctional personality, recognize there's dysfunction in you.

ALLOWANCES

In the next section, I'll describe *personality traits* to help you identify your player. Before I do, I want to reiterate that you are not to judge your player. You are to observe and recognize only. To judge promotes negative behavior aligned with the rules. Stay focused to eliminate your ego. Be careful, do not become the judge and jury. Keep in mind that judgment is an assessment based on assumptions without evidence or inquiry. To judge will often result in wrong conclusions. Avoid the knee-jerk reaction to prematurely judge your player. You are to only observe while each move confirms the answer. Be humble in your own self-awareness.

When your player judges, recognize his insecurities. Watch for the defense. Your observation requires patience without saying a word. When it's your turn, your response must be a direct response to your player's move, not a random response with no relevance to the points made. Stay on topic. When you watch closely, you'll notice that your player's personality reveals a *lot before you get to the next gate*—which is to recognize his intelligence. More often, your player's personality will lead to a lost King even if you miss the physical cues from the first gate.

Each gate builds upon the next. If your player's appearance is not to your liking, acknowledge and accept, and continue to watch closely. Look for the value in your player. If you're struggling to pick up on his vibration, the next gate will provide more clues. If you fail to recognize how his personality is breaking the rules, you will get hurt. Be careful not to let your ego tell you to make *allowances* for the red flags that you see. The Game teaches us how to become trustworthy and who to trust. Be honest with yourself. If you don't trust your player, evidenced by a lack of character, it's game over. If you deny the evidence, know that you're serving your ego; fear. Consequently, you can't be trusted either. If your player can't be trusted and you can't be trusted, nothing good will come of your relationship. Whatever your plans are together, they *will* come to a painful end.

Observe your player carefully. A master player will see truth within the personality gate. As a beginner, you will feel uncomfortable in their presence. Professional and non-professional counselors, and coaches, label "dysfunction" as a "personality disorder." If a player reveals to you terms like 'bi-polar', 'multiple personality disorder', 'ADD', 'ADHD', 'narcissist', 'gas-lighter', and 'schizophrenic' to name a few, these descriptions all belong within the personality gate. You don't have to be a professional to know that you instinctively don't trust these types of players. These traits are an automatic game over. You will get hurt by the troubled player. Do not trust this player with your heart, beliefs, well-being, advice, or money. They will disappoint you.

When you make *allowances* for dysfunctional personalities, you are in agreement with the assault against your Spirit. You confirm your lack of self-love and inadvertently acknowledge the division between you and God. Without self-love, you are dangerous to others. With self-love, you maintain boundaries. Without boundaries, you break the rules and hurt your player. *Do not hurt your player.* Self-awareness is infinitely more important than defending yourself against a loveless player. Life will grant you favor when you maintain honor, enduring the hit to your ego. Favor is not granted to those who cause pain to others. When you make allowances whether for yourself or others, know that pain will follow.

The following list of *personality traits* are included to help you recognize the behaviors described as the second gate. These identifiers help you to distinguish between personality and character. They are not to be used as accusations to demean your player. Study them closely to understand how certain personality traits will either keep you engaged enough to get you to the next gate, or they will be an automatic game over.

ABUSIVE	ACCUSER	ADAPTABLE	AGREEABLE
ALCOHOLIC	ALLURING	ANNOYING	APPALLING
ARROGANT	ARTICULATE	ARTISTIC	ATTENTION SEEKING
ATTENTIVE	BACKSTABBER	BLUNT	BOASTFUL
BOISTEROUS	BOLD	BOSSY	BRAVE
BRAZEN	BRIGHT	BROKE (MENTALITY)	BROWN-NOSER
BUBBLY	CARING	CAUTIOUS	CHEAP
COMBATIVE	COMPLAINER	CONNECTOR	CONSIDERATE
CONTEMPLATIVE	CONTRARY	COOL	CRABBY
CRASS ROUGH	CREATIVE	CRUDE	CURIOUS
CYNICAL	DECEITFUL	DECEIVING	DECENT
DEEP	DEFIANT	DELICATE	DELICATE
DEMANDING	DEMEANING	DENIAL	DETERMINED
DICTATOR	DIGNIFIED	DIRTY	DISGUSTING
DISRESPECTFUL	DISTASTEFUL	DOWNER	DRAMA

DREAMER	DRIVEN	DRY	EASY-GOING
EDGY	EGOTISTICAL	ENTHUSIASTIC	ENTITLED
EXPERIENCED	EXTRAVAGANT	EXTROVERT	FAIR
FASHIONABLE	FATALIST	FEARFUL	FEMININE
FLAMBOYANT	FLIPPANT	FOLLOWER	FUNNY
GENEROUS	GIDDY	GIFTED	GOSSIPER
GULLIBLE	HAPPY	HARD WORKER	HARSH
HIP	HONEST	HOSPITABLE	HURTFUL
HYPER	HYSTERICAL	IMPOSING	IMPRESSIVE
INCONSIDERATE	INNOCENT	INQUISITIVE	INSECURE
INSULTING	INTIMIDATING	INTROVERT	INTRUSIVE
JOKESTER	JUDGMENTAL	KIND	KNOW-IT-ALL
KNOWLEDGEABLE	LAZY	LEADER	LIAR
LIKABLE	LOSER	LOUD	LOVING
MANIPULATIVE	MASCULINE	MEEK	MOTIVATED
MOTIVATING	MYSTERIOUS	NAME CALLER	NEEDY
NEGATIVE	NERVOUS	OBSTINATE	OFFENSIVE
OPPORTUNIST	PEOPLE PLEASER	PERFECTIONIST	PERSISTENT
PICKY	PLANNER	POLISHED	POLITICAL
POOR	POPULAR	POSITIVE	PRAGMATIC
PRESUMPTUOUS	PRETENTIOUS	PRIDEFUL	PRIVATE
PROBLEM SOLVER	PROUD	PRUDE	REACTIVE
REALIST	RELIGIOUS	RESPONSIVE	RISK TAKER
SAD	SAFE	SALESMAN	SARCASTIC
SASSY	SCARY	SCORE KEEPER	SELF-DEPRECATING
SELF-INFLATED	SELFISH	SELFLESS	SHALLOW
SHORT TEMPERED	SHOW OFF	SHYSTER	SILLY
SIMPLE	SLY	SNARKY	SOFT SPOKEN
SOLID	SOMBER	SPIRITUAL	SPONTANEOUS
STRATEGIC	STRIKING	STRONG	SUBSERVIENT
TAKER	TALENTED	TALKER	THREATENING
TOUGH	TWO-FACED	UNAWARE	UNCOOPERATIVE
UNDERHANDED	UNDERSTANDING	UNMOTIVATED	UNREFINED
VIRTUOUS	VISIONARY	WEAK	WEALTHY
WELCOMING	WILLING	WISE	WITTY

The list is not exhaustive, but you get the picture with the adjectives that describe personality.

Personality Is Not Character

This is the part where most people get confused about their player because the first and second gate appear to encompass the entirety of who they are. If your player is fairly attractive and has a personality that is agreeable and funny, their good qualities will tend to speak for their character, but, only in the beginning. Be careful, this is where allowances start to slide on a slippery slope. It's natural to want to see the good in your player but seeing the good can quickly turn to tolerating reactive behavior. Tolerating reactive behavior is self-sacrifice. A master player knows that a reactive player breaks the rules, sometimes casually, other times more seriously without boundary. The inexperienced player tolerates poor behavior and will continue until the bitter end instead of seeing the road ahead and calling game over. The ego will convince you that you can handle the misbehavior until your player changes their behavior. The problem is your *tolerance* and *patience* coupled with your expectation for change (virtues and a rule combined) translates to an unspoken contract, where you acknowle and accept your player as they are. There is no motivation for change.

The Ego Is Self-Serving

The ego is weak when it's time to make tough decisions. The ego tells you to withstand the abuse and take pride in your endurance. Be aware that the devil's presence shines bright in the personality gate. Your player's personality is susceptible to the dark force that controls his worldly desires and self-image. Knowing this, you not only have to watch your player, but you also have to be careful to recognize where the devil is taking over in *your mind* too. It's easy to succumb to the idea that nobody's perfect. Complacency says, "It's easier to make allowances for the wrong player than to maintain my boundary to love myself first." The challenge to maintain the boundary becomes too difficult. Self-respect is lost. The ego has your mind going around in circles as you try to find reasons to stay with your player because leaving the table poses a risk when you're not absolute in your conviction.

THE DEVIL IS RUTHLESS

He will remind you of all the reasons why you hate your player when you're in play; then he'll turn around and remind you of all the reasons why you love your player when you find the strength to walk away. Self-doubt has you trapped when you don't know your value. The devil will cripple your conviction to love yourself first. If you want to master The Game, it's imperative to know that you will always choose yourself. Period. You can't get soft if you are to be the guardian of the gate. The ego lives in the world, the Holy Spirit lives in you. Serve the Holy Spirit or serve the world.

To love yourself is to *elevate your standards* while *maintaining your boundaries.* Let's clarify to understand the difference. When you have high standards, you commit to honorable and virtuous behavior. To have high standards is not to hold an expectation that others must meet your desire for a physically attractive player who has a shining personality, and a junk drawer full of certificates and qualifications to meet your financial expectations. In The Game, *a standard sets the bar* for *your* behavior. Standards are *vertical,* boundaries are *horizontal. Standards* keep you accountable to the Most High, *the boundary* is the line drawn where you don't break the rules regardless of how deserving your player. Draw the line, stay on your side of the board to align with God's favor.

Personality is often confused with character because the word character is used to describe personality. Think of actors playing their role as a cowboy, ballerina, bad boy, and sexpot, or mysterious, comedic, and romantic. It's a personality they play. Character is virtue.

The Game will reveal the truth about every player as if naked. Every thought, motive, and behavior becomes very clear when you wear the armor of God.

P*art 22*

THE THIRD GATE

INTELLIGENCE

"He" is used to generalize the word "player" for simplicity.

Intelligence is a delicate subject. This is the part where the ego stands up and says, "I've got this," but then the ego proceeds to cast judgment as the information proves to be challenging and appears to be downright offensive. Naturally, the line of defense is to judge the author of the content instead of being objective to the value of the insight. The ego will try to object to the validity of the information, reducing it down to a single perspective. Be open to the information and ask for clear understanding.

The Messiah says, "I am the way, the truth, and the life." John 14:6. The Messiah is the way and the weigh. The greatest measure of power will forever be Love. There is only one truth. If it's not love, it's not true. The Messiah is the life. Life is the creative unseen; the field of love energy. The field of love energy is consciousness. Consciousness is the one supreme, omniscient mind. Simply put, if you want to elevate from human intelligence to *Spiritually Enlightened,* you'll want to be humble, surrender your ego, and ask for understanding.

Now that we know how to recognize *physical attributes,* and *identify personality,* next is to understand *The Five Levels of Intelligence. The Third Gate* helps you to identify how the devil controls behavior through our ignorance of love. Be careful not to make allowances for your player's appearance and personality when you're bedazzled by his intelligence. The first two gates give clues about your player's character. His intelligence becomes irrelevant if he loses his King within the first two gates. If you miss the clues, your ability to use your virtues will be challenged by your player's intelligence. Virtue trumps intelligence. But, if you don't have your pieces on the board, you will naturally lean on his knowledge and reasoning without picking up on the broken rules. Ignorance is Satan's trap.

If you succumb to a subordinate position, you are no longer actively playing your side of the board. Your player will control you as you lose sight of the rules and pieces, forgetting to pause, be objective and ask questions. If you fail to regain the concept of The Game, you'll revert back to your old behaviors. Pain is inevitable. If he can impress you with his knowledge and an income that supports the evidence of his knowledge, you will easily be susceptible to the path of destruction. Be careful not to *blindly trust* your educated player. Education is not an indication of good character. Do not believe that your player has honor and integrity when he impresses you with his learned vocabulary. Learn to put *all* your faith in knowing how to move your pieces. Your ability to love (move with virtue) will *always* protect you. The truth about your player will come to light before you get hurt. Trust in your ability to play the game. The formula never fails. Your heart, money, and honor will be safe when you're accountable to God (love) first. Where there is love, there is no risk. Where there is ego, everything's at risk. Satan has no mercy.

FIVE LEVELS OF INTELLIGENCE

The path to Enlightenment.

The Five Levels of Intelligence describe human consciousness with respect to a loving behavior. The world is filled with *intelligent* players who, in their disillusionment, continue to be the cause of pain to themself and others. The ego will be offended by the following descriptions, while the spirit will be inspired to go higher. The player with all the pieces reaches enlightenment.

UNEDUCATED

The following description is not to categorize the less fortunate who, for whatever reason, failed to have the opportunity to go to school. Rather, it's to describe the unpolished, ignorant individual who fails to have even the slightest understanding about the behavior of love. *The uneducated player* represents the "wide path," *the largest population* residing at the lowest level of consciousness; the lowest vibration known as the cesspool. The player residing at the lowest level of consciousness does not have the awareness to recognize the need for personal development, to master his ego, improve his spirituality, be accountable, or elevate his consciousness in order to transform himself through the power of love. Although he may be familiar with the vocabulary, he struggles to embody the words he cannot define. His evolution, therefore, is obstructed by his lack of interest to improve his education. To the uneducated player love is simple, dismissed as common knowledge. His egotistical and ignorant existence lacks self-awareness, which makes him opinionated, offensive, defensive, entitled, willful, uncooperative, racist, self-righteous and narrow-minded as his short-sighted perception of life is determined by a simple, low vibrational level of understanding. He will fail to recognize or respect the player who has an elevated conscience, behaving according to virtue, having boundaries and standards.

The *uneducated player* will internalize his insecurities and over compensate with offensive behavior as he breaks the rules with impatience, defense, conflict, aggressiveness, hostility, belligerence and arrogance. He will manipulate his player with ultimatums, mind games, guilt, ridicule, and false promises. The uneducated player is prone to anger as he struggles to communicate effectively. Without effective communication, his reactions turn to violence, using physical and mental abuse to express his untamed emotions. The uneducated player is ignorant to the ways of love and ignorant to the presence of God. The uneducated player *will* break the rules and you *will* get hurt. The uneducated player has no comprehension, consideration, or respect for God's glory or the magnificent Oneness of creation. He fails to honor or care for his brother, nature, animals, and himself. He'll destroy at will and kill without reason or remorse. He's lazy, having no perception of his lack of contribution, while at the same time feeling entitled to the first fruits of others. He's an opportunist without respect for his player. He lacks a moral compass and thinks others are no better. He believes his player is just as guilty and behaves the same way. His inability to recognize when others have sacrificed on his behalf prevents him from forming true relationships.

The uneducated, ignorant player has no filter, and will say anything he pleases, entitled to his opinion no matter the consequence. The ignorant player will deny probable cause without research or having any knowledge of the subject in question. He plays devil's advocate without caring about the integrity of the discussion or the relationship. He's a contrarian, never knowing how or when to acknowledge and accept what his player is conveying. The ignorant player sees division in the world around him. He stands alone as he competes for his space, believing everyone is against him. He believes in Karma, but not in God's favor. He wants something for nothing, thinking the world owes him for all of his suffering, holding no accountability for his own decisions. The ignorant player blames everyone else for his life of consequences. He accuses without cause or before asking questions. He believes he is the judge and jury, authorized to control the will of others. He uses force, intimidation, and threats to control the player he feels is different. Be it the color of their skin, ethnicity, religion, sex, political affiliation, baseball team or any other three dimensional world view that creates a perception of division. The ignorant player is victim to Satan's domain, honoring money before God, himself, and others. His narrow-minded view believes he is intelligent, having common sense and struggles to understand why others prove to be idiots. With an ego as dirty as the swamp, he is the lowest and furthest distance from the Most High vibration. His weak and cowardly behavior makes him easy to identify and makes it easy for you to call game over.

EDUCATED

The *educated player* is your *most dangerous player* that requires your focused attention to avoid being hurt. First, allow me to explain the difference between being disappointed and being hurt by your player. Understand that you will be *disappointed* with your player's behavior 1) because you have *expectations* and 2) because your player doesn't know The Game. When you've been *hurt* by your player, there's an element of betrayal, gossip, theft, abuse, infidelity, manipulation, ultimatums, an absence of boundaries combined with low standards. Your energetic connection is severed when your player crosses the line, breaks the rules and fails to maintain his king on the board. *A violated boundary is an unprovoked and unwarranted act against your will.* When your player cheats, his move requires you to make a move that you don't necessarily want to make. Had he not cheated, you wouldn't have to call game over. It's not an easy decision. Many people make allowances in exchange for a *promise* to "never do it again," opting to continue playing the game. This will prove to be a regretful decision. Don't expect change for the future when the past proves the character. When it's your move, you must choose between self-sacrifice, making *allowances* for your player by "forgiving" him, or maintaining a high *standard* for yourself by acknowledging that the game is over. If you can't trust him, the King is off the board. Game Over. The relationship will come to an end even if you don't officially call game over because your energetic tie is broken, leaving you to drift apart until you finally walk away. The sin cannot escape the field of truth. Your love energy will continue to divide until you can no longer deny your truth.

When you forgive, the forgiveness must be an act of love toward yourself, not a dismissal for your player's behavior. It's only when you *blame* and play the *victim* are you positioned to assume you have the authority to forgive your player. In The Game, there can be no victim or blame. With no victim or someone to blame, there's nothing left to forgive. The correct move is to *acknowledge* and *accept* their move (behavior-cheating), then exercise *grace* and *mercy.* Speak with a graceful tongue and maintain your honor by not giving what is deserved; instead, give an undeserved, kind dismissal. If you use forgiveness as a means to avoid your responsibility to make a tough decision, know that you're only making allowances with the expectation that he keeps his word to change. If your player had *integrity* from the start, there would be no reason for you to make allowances because your player wouldn't put you in a position to call game over. Recognize the integrity of your player. Should you choose to deny and make excuses, your relationship will not continue in love. Once the infidelity is committed, it's too late whether or not your player keeps his word. Any promise for change becomes irrelevant because your trust is broken. Like a broken pane of glass, it will never be the same. People don't change just because they get caught cheating. To forgive means you accept the breach of contract coupled with an *expectation* for change. Energetically, you *lower your intrinsic value*, taking a hit to your self-worth. You are not to sacrifice your self-worth for the benefit of your player. There's no incentive for him to change. Maintain your post as guardian of the gate and call game over.

Many times, a relationship is over long before it ends because you keep making allowances and excuses to avoid the tough decision. When it finally ends, the pain from your broken heart is much more severe and regretful because you continued to trust your player who couldn't be trusted from the beginning. For this reason, you need the strength and courage to make tough decisions. Commit to love yourself *first*. Your aim is to be one with God to live in favor. If you are to *be love* and reach the Most High vibration, you must choose to love yourself first with every move no matter the sacrifice or blow to your ego. Imagine that you have one choice, to honor the player in front of you or to honor your relationship with the one above you. Always choose the one above you. Your relationship with God always comes first because it's the only one you can count on to deliver.

The educated player is a product of social engineering who has followed the system that requires him to attain diplomas, degrees and certificates. The time he's invested prepares him for corporate employment, higher wages, taxes, debt, and a seat at the table with his socioeconomic peers. The educated player is thrown onto the ladder of success with accumulated knowledge relating to his field. Once educated, this player rarely makes time to learn the ways of love or *how* to be *one with God*. His focus is directed at how to increase financially. Although he may be part of a church congregation, he's too busy taking care of responsibilities to take time out to learn about himself and his true super power within. The remainder of his education is acquired through life experience, balancing work, family, church and financial obligations as needed. Life and money drive the educated player. The power of love is not his concern. His life experience presents enough obstacles and opportunity to use his education consisting of logic, reason, and deduction to keep him occupied and entertained while keeping him on the cycle of the material illusion.

Evidence of love in his life is demonstrated through friends, family, and children. The educated player believes he is intelligent enough to understand what love is and so he "wings it" having no real concept. He, like others, accept that nobody's perfect. Besides, love is easy when you have money. Those with money find that "love" comes easy because the ego is infatuated with the material world. The educated mind is the devil's playground. The ego takes pride in title, fame, fortune, status, and money. The educated player acquires quite the junk drawer full of accomplishments, trophies, diplomas, certificates, cars, houses, clothes, jewelry, and everything money can buy to impress his player and cover what he's hiding. His junk drawer becomes a mask as he hides the truth about his character. Don't assume his honor and integrity are in place because he's been "blessed" with an impressive collection of material possessions according to an earthly perspective. Don't be fooled. The educated player with all his riches will never be more valuable than the player who learns how to love, being blessed with God's favor. The educated player, in his ignorance, will produce unnecessary chaos and drama within his relationships. He will continue to break the rules with all of his players in just a few moves. The educated player perpetuates the cycle of broken homes, emotional dysfunction, and personality disorders. His method of operation is aligned with a programmed mentality that serves the holographic world that honors money.

The educated player is your most dangerous player because their junk drawer of material wealth and pedigree gives them an impressive vocabulary, associations, and affiliations which serves to feed the ego by inflating their intelligence quotient. You'll find that they are arrogant enough to put you in your place should there be conflict instead of having patience, diplomacy, and grace to deliver the same message. Their arrogant sense of value and autonomy gives them the courage to dismiss and disrespect without care or consequence. When your player is educated, you'll notice their affinity to playing devil's advocate, even when they have no concern or knowledge of the topic. They are ignorant to the consequence of their actions. They insult the uneducated and challenge the highly educated. Their smart self-image believes they are equal, if not superior. The educated player knows enough to act like he knows everything, being contrary to your point instead of acknowledging and accepting. This player is prone to attachment, jealousy, manipulation, retaliation, arrogance, guilt, insults, name calling, and rule breaking as they fail to align their behavior with virtue. Their love is conditional, often reverting to an eye for an eye. Their relationships are built on benefits, expectations, agreements, unspoken contracts, exceptions, excuses, blame, and pride. In simpler terms: drama.

The adage, "nobody's perfect," becomes the crutch for their less-than-honorable standard of behavior. The educated player often exhibits an average, middle-of-the-road moral compass. When it comes to admirable behavior, this player likes to fly by the seat of their pants. You'll witness conflicting values dependent on the situation instead of watching them maintain the same set of values regardless of the situation. Of course, the educated player would not describe themselves this way, as most believe they are good people because they pride themselves on meeting social standards. Meeting these standards somehow defaults to the assumption of knowing what love is. It doesn't. If you find yourself being triggered by the seemingly unjust opinion and judgment of the description, I suggest you pay close attention to the mirror. If you feel the need to defend yourself with loopholes, justifications, and denials, ask yourself why you want to reject what is being illuminated. If you are the educated player, you believe you're well-informed and qualified to challenge the narrative because the ego naturally wants to find fault in the messenger instead of considering the truth in the message. The challenge is to be objective about the reality of your behavior.

Back to recognizing your player. Once you discern the level of your player's intelligence, you'll be confident to slow down and play without rushing in to a relationship of any kind. Enjoy learning how to recognize these five levels of intelligence and the motivation for the behavior. Take every opportunity to use your pieces. When you become a focused player, you'll benefit from each move as well as receive unexpected favor from the universe. Be careful not to hand over your heart (trust) before identifying the Five Gates in your player. If you do, you will definitely get hurt. Play your side of the board using only virtue with focus, patience, and intention. No matter how attractive or charismatic your player, you must stay objective in order to recognize the level of their intelligence. Smart, witty, funny, sexy, and fun can get you in trouble when you fail to recognize your player's inability to love. Stick to the rules and pieces. Don't ditch the proven formula for success because you're attracted to your player and your player shows an interest in you. Respect your position as the Gate Keeper. You are responsible even when you don't take responsibility. Your decisions will immediately result in favor or consequence. Watch yourself carefully to maintain your boundary to not break the rules, and keep your standard of behavior to only responding with virtue. Self-discipline is imperative as it will stop your fleeting emotions from "falling in love."

Love is a behavior, not an emotion. Your players appearance and behavior will often be attractive and charming enough for you to forget about the consequence of your ignorance. Slow the game down by taking your time to identify the gates, sharpen your awareness of the rules, and make *one virtuous move at a time.* The universe will reveal your player's character, as well as yours. Your relationship with the educated player is a test, exposing your commitment to love and your loyalty to elevating to the Most High vibration. Listen more, say less, and protect your King.

Show a genuine interest in your player. Stay neutral and objective as you get to know each other's method of operation. Your behavior is priority before proving yourself "right" if you are to remain in good graces with our Father. Do not try to change your player's character. Let him be responsible for his own game. Let him make his own decision about his moves. Do not be foolish to think that you have the power to change your player's character. You don't. You will be hurt and disappointed because *character is built not imposed.* You can only *improve on your own* character and *recognize* the character of your player. Your *strongest move* with the educated player is to *acknowledge and accept* their move *first* before using another virtue. Each time you're able to acknowledge and accept, you control the board and the direction of your player's next move. The temperaments will remain amicable and respectful during the process of understanding each other.

So why is the educated player your most dangerous player? Because they are most often a beautiful soul, friendly, helpful, and considerate. They welcome you with a smile, shake your hand, and will often give you hug. They listen to your problems, offer advice, and administer "tough" love. They teach you things you don't know and are respectful of your opinion. They host gatherings, watch your kids, and cry at the same movies. They pick you up when you're down and give you a shoulder to cry on. The educated player often fails to respect you and your education, but will also protect, support, and even fight to the death for you. They'll support your cause with generosity, be selfless, and proactive. The educated player is considered to be a friend, so you're willing to make allowances for their behavior. They're smooth talkers, rational, and respectable. They're innovators, dreamers, and motivational speakers. The educated player is polished, someone you look up to. They're preachers, teachers, doctors, philosophers, you name it. The danger lies in their good-hearted intentions coupled with a polished appearance and educated mannerisms that create a fog of mental and emotional confusion with their player. You want to trust them. The educated player is intelligent enough to use logic, reason, critical thinking, and 'normal' behavior to make you believe they are accountable and conscious enough to do no harm. Assuming this is true, you will release your guard, become vulnerable and believe that your heart and valuables are held in Trust. Beware. Favorable personality traits mask the truth of missing virtues. Without virtue, you can't trust the educated player. In a moment and without warning, they will rip your heart out, having no boundary or self-respect, breaking your trust without remorse or a change in behavior. The educated player will expect to be forgiven. It's too late. The King is lost. Any expectation for the relationship to improve will result in disappointment and more pain. It's inevitable. In the end, you'll have to forgive yourself for choosing to sacrifice your self-worth instead of maintaining your standard of self-love.

HIGHLY EDUCATED

The highly educated player possesses uncommon knowledge. Somehow in some way, he's been exposed to intelligent operations. He knows the workings of processes, history, figures, numbers, etymology, philosophy, beliefs, and the difference between fact and opinion. He's studied and educated above common understanding. His perceptions are far beyond the simple conversations that entertain the educated. He's a lone wolf, un-relatable to the educated and uneducated player. His mind and imagination are filled with valuable information waiting for the moment to engage in intellectual grapple. The highly educated player is a watcher, complacent about superficial beauty and materialism. His perception of others is low as most prove to disappoint him. He's not interested in the theatrics of self-inflicted drama from those claiming the sky is falling. The highly educated player has mastered his logic and reason. He's able to discern the emotionally triggered player, watching from the sidelines with amusement.

In his relationships, he's experienced heartbreak many times. Love has proven to be an ideal or fairytale. In reality it's a lot of work. The story always seems to end the same. Once the romance is over, you're lucky if you can remain friends. The highly educated player lacks the emotion, energy, and passion necessary to ignite new relationships. Often times, this player will be comfortably settled in with a long-term partner. The two have become comfortably autonomous in their own existence. New relationships may be entertained, but with minimal effort to actively involve themself in a new environment. The highly educated player is the old dog who's not interested in learning new tricks. He doesn't want to learn about love, implement a silly game, or be expected to adhere to rules in a relationship. Although they may be amused, and even entertained, the idea of life being magical is an unquantifiable fairytale not worth the effort. Why risk being disappointed? Unfortunately, the adversary has planted a seed of doubt in every possibility, making the highly educated require factual evidence before effort is put forward.

The highly educated player without virtuous character is a wicked player. It's imperative that you discern where virtue is missing early in the game before becoming vulnerable to their impressive intelligence. Keep in mind that you don't need to elevate your intelligence to balance his, so don't feel threatened. Your goal is to keep your king on the board. Remain in honor. Once you identify that your player is highly educated, and witness which pieces are missing from his board, you'll know if he can be trusted. Watch and listen for the rules being broken. Each rule of ill behavior has a substitute virtuous behavior. The move is a choice of free will. Love or not to love. Watch carefully. Should he lose his king, you must still maintain your honor in the relationship. You must have clean hands, even when the game is over. Take the high road knowing the universe is watching every decision you and your player make. Stay in favor. The highly educated player may not intentionally set out to hurt you, but he may be an opportunist who cares nothing about integrity or consequence.

SELF-EDUCATED

The self-educated player is focused on his own interests and the interests of his player. Those who take an interest in educating themselves further than what's offered in school often find themselves down a rabbit hole as Spirit opens the door to a whole new world. One thing leads to another when the heart is free to follow the call. The more he learns, the more there is to learn. His search is endless as the heart directs his path to self-actualization. A man's drive to attain more knowledge is infinite until he realizes that the knowledge he seeks is the same energy directing him to know God. Love is the way, the life, and the truth. His innate desire to understand his purpose in the grand scheme of things is to know his maker. God is Love. When he knows what love is, he will know God and he will have found the key to his happiness and fulfillment. There is no higher, more worthy or fulfilling aspiration than to know what love is.

The self-educated player is overwhelmed by the immense amount of uncharted knowledge he's yet to learn. He's humbled by his ignorance. A humble player is not a threat. A humble player seeks to know more and will devote his time to reading and cross referencing to satisfy his insatiable appetite for answers. The self-educated player is fascinated by the vastness of information provided by the universe. He submits and allows the Spirit to move him in the direction of his curiosity without concern of what others will think of him. With the acknowledgment of the Spirit, he becomes a servant to the universe as each desire and curiosity is answered. His compassion grows as he recognizes the value in himself, others and in nature. He accepts with gratitude everything God has created in the world and he respects it.

What the self-educated player most often fails to do is be one with the creator. His identity is held hostage by worldly views that perpetuate the idea that he is separate from that which he's made of. The ego will use guilt when he tries to claim the purity of God, and use fear to create the illusion of consequence. The ego tempers his power, keeping him in fear of overstepping his boundary. When the ego is in play, you, as his player, are in danger. Although the self-educated player believes he's a good person, innocent from hurting others, his illusion of being separate from his creator makes him susceptible to the ego. If he fails to see himself as God, he won't act like God (love). This is the gap between him and the enlightened. The self-educated player sees himself in his brother and in nature, but he fails to see himself as God, as well as failing to see God in others and in nature. He is a man and God is his superior. He and God are divided. As long as his ego remains, he will fail to reach the highest vibrational power. He can't serve both God and ego.

The way for you to identify the self-educated player is to recognize his relationship with money. Money represents the material world ruled by the ego. The fear of not having money is the cause of unloving behavior. Self-concern, accounting, fairness, checks and balances, perceived value vs. benefit, and a broke mentality is the egos method of control. Watch your player carefully when he makes decisions. In everything he does, there's only one choice. He will either make decisions based on money, or he will make decisions based on love. There's no straddling the fence. Should he choose money, know that eventually you will get hurt if you continue to trust him. The self-educated player strives to know rather than to be, and so, fails to rid himself of his emotional controller—the puppeteer known as the devil. When in doubt, follow the money. Watch how your player places his priority on the importance of a frugal money mindset, and fairness in the material world. Anytime your player places money before relationships, you'll witness him breaking the rules. Look for signs contrary to virtuous behavior. Money arguments sound like assumptions, expectations, accusations, blame, and defense. Honorable money talk will acknowledge and accept, exhibit faith, patience, and respect for his player.

ENLIGHTENED

The enlightened player is a player for keeps. Should you be so blessed to come into his presence, you must quickly and consciously elevate your self-awareness. Be sure to remember your virtues, behave with grace, transparency, and respect. The enlightened player will recognize you immediately. His consciousness will read your vibration, see through your insecurities, identify your motives, and be extremely perceptive to the ways and desires of your ego. The way to remain in play with the enlightened player is to become equally yoked with the same honest and transparent heart-centered vibration. Any show of arrogance, righteousness, inauthentic, superficial behavior will be received like a radio wave long before the introduction. He will not subject himself to the antics of the thoughtless and reactive moves made by the egotistical player who is controlled by the world of fear, scarcity, urgency, poverty, popularity, and status. He will walk away from the board before you realize that you were in play. The enlightened player plays the most elevated game, being conscious of his moves on many boards at the same time knowing how they affect each other. He's mastered self-discipline, having the highest respect for his commitment to virtuous behavior. His accountability to being one with love makes him your most loyal and trusted player. If you fail to recognize him, you'll lose this invaluable lifelong friend.

To better understand the enlightened player, we start by recognizing which virtuous behaviors are shown in your player's personality, intellect, and character. The enlightened player controls the board with a natural sense of peace and security about him. There's no drama. He does not react under pressure when his player has an emotional outbreak or tantrum. He won't defend himself. He seeks to understand his player objectively without taking offense. He controls the board. He doesn't force his voice to be heard, but instead exercises patience, waiting for his turn. His boundaries are clear with full intention to keep his King firmly on the board. He's not afraid of his player's move, allowing him to be independent in thought and behavior. He does not bully his player to convert to his own ideas and perceptions. He will often recognize his player's indiscretions with other players, cover for him when the opportunity rises, then speak with him privately.

The educated player will often judge the enlightened player by the way he understands himself instead of being skilled to recognize his player's virtuous behavior. The educated player's level of understanding and awareness prevents him from seeing the difference between himself and his enlightened player. The educated player looks for common interests between himself and others. He looks for personality traits, hobbies, beliefs, and physical attributes to determine whether they have found an equitable relationship, where the enlightened player has an intimate relationship with God in himself and recognizes others who have the same, being equally yoked. The enlightened player is secure in his oneness with God. He knows that love is the Most High vibration and is committed to it. His spirit does not look for loyalty from his player on a horizontal plane, instead, he looks for vertical accountability between his player and God. Accountability to God makes him loyal to the One and not to the player. Loyalty to the One is how you will know it's safe to Trust.

The enlightened player is not concerned about how his player will behave. He's confident in his ability to move his virtues with relevance and ease. He's mastered the art of accepting what is presented without interference, knowing he'll make the right move when it's his turn. He knows the first move is to acknowledge and accept. Self-discipline is the key. The ease of his game is often misunderstood to the ego-driven player. He can't put his finger on what makes the Enlightened player so fortunate and care free. The enlightened player plays at the highest elevation. He immerses himself in all that is good, beautiful, righteous, and noble. His life is a canvas where all of creation is a brush stroke from God's creative hand in everything. He respects mother earth and cares for those who rely upon her. He is one with the animals, the garden, music, the sea and humanity. He lives in gratitude for all that is created. You can be certain the enlightened player will never hurt you. If you lose your King, he will walk away leaving you to endure the pain of his absence. What about forgiveness, you might be wondering? The enlightened player is never the victim, nor does he blame his player for behaving the way he does. Instead, he will graciously acknowledge the level of play and accept the ignorance of his player knowing he has room to grow. The enlightened player will never hurt or retaliate. He will continue to be respectful although knowing his player is not to be trusted.

Part 23

THE FOURTH GATE

CHARACTER

The fourth gate is character. The board is complete with all the pieces. Like an onion with many layers, character is at the core of your player. The core of your player is his true self, prior to reaching the essence of spirit. Character is a constant, where looks, personality, and intelligence may change as time passes. Your player may change his style, likes, dislikes, grow in maturity, and learn new things, but his character will never change while you're in play. If he hurts you once, he'll hurt you twice and over again. Those who make promises need to be observed closely. In truth, when a player knows who he is and knows his standards, his moves are purposeful so there's no need for promises to come later. When you hear that "people don't change," believe it when you're in play.

Unlike personality and appearance, character is built upon morals, values, and ethics consistently demonstrated alone and with his player. Without having a role model to solidify his understanding of honor and integrity, the world around him will teach him to mirror what's acceptable to the collective. It's then up to the individual to decide whether he will be accountable to an elevated standard of values. Those who are without the building blocks for noble character will get old, irrelevant, and unattractive to their player instead of aging gracefully. To age gracefully, you must set your intentions on loving harder. Loving harder is to push yourself to purposely love on your player by being virtuous in order to create experiences that may not have otherwise occurred. This is the secret to long lasting relationships.

The list of virtues provides a road map for extraordinary character development. When you push yourself to practice voicing the unexpected and demonstrating purposeful acts of kindness, you will fall in love with the beauty in you. The more reasons you give yourself to be proud of your behavior, the more gratitude you'll experience and the more universal favor you'll receive. Anyone wanting success with their relationships must remember this, most people won't care about what you've done until they care about who you are. When your character leaves an impression, what you've accomplished becomes of interest.

$Part$ 24

THE FIFTH GATE

SPIRITUALITY

Spirituality in the purest form is a oneness with the unseen. The unseen exists in you, it's the breath of life. The breath of life in you is the creator of that which is seen. Spirituality is your breath, one with the unseen, unified without definition, condition or boundary. Your breath is your Spirit. Your Spirit communicates with the unseen Holy Spirit, and is the reason why the answer to all of your questions lie within you. There is no separation between you and the All. There is only the illusion of separation. The condition, whether human, plant, or animal, gives the illusion of separation from the Holy Spirit, but the Holy Spirit cannot be separated. All is one, and the One is All.

To be spiritual is a choice by those who do not resonate with the controlling faction of religion. When recognizing your player, do not assume that the spiritual player and the religious player are the same. They are not. Watch the difference in behavior. The spiritual player is much like the enlightened player in that they both go within for answers knowing that they are one with Spirit. The religious player is divided between himself and that which is outside of himself. The religious player leans on ego where the Spirirtual player leans on love. You'll recognize their game by how easily they get offended, using scripture to defend their position with conviction instead of demonstrating love.

The player who claims to be spiritual must be watched carefully, as many fail to be true. Pay attention to their behavior. Spirituality is not spiritual when its personality. The personality of the self-proclaimed "spiritual" looks like yoga, crystals, chants, singing bowls, sage, one love mantras, and meditation. They say things like 'namaste' and bow after their poses. They dress in flowing clothes, flat shoes and beaded bracelets around their wrists. Vegan is the lifestyle along with incense and fluted music. I don't give this description to discriminate or to judge, but rather to identify what spirituality is not. Spirituality is not appearances; in fact, it is an abomination when the connection to the Holy Spirit is missing. The truly spiritual player may or may not have the same qualities in their personality. His personality can be very simple as his connection to spirit does not require outward appearances to his peers. Watch his behavior. The spiritual personality is controlled by ego, where the truly spiritual player is one with love.

When you've mastered your Ego, using only your pieces, and find yourself happy, peaceful, and grateful for the power you now hold, you will have reached Spiritual Enlightenment.

Part 25

FORGIVENESS, CHANCES, AND TRUST

"How do you recognize a lifelong player?
He is equally yoked in character."

~Princess Merrilee of Solana

In The Game, forgiveness is a virtue. It is a virtue because it's important to forgive yourself for the mistakes you've made—especially when you come to realize the damage you've caused to those you love. As your understanding becomes clearer to the workings of The Game, you'll see how forgiveness and chances are almost the same. It's important to detach from the idea of forgiveness being something you gift to your player. To forgive implies authority. The only authority you have is over yourself. You have the power to release your own pain. Your player can't do that for you. Even when your player says, "I forgive you," it's not enough if you fail to forgive yourself for the mistakes you've made. Forgiveness is a gift to yourself.

If you have "forgiven" someone, you will most likely agree, forgiveness turns to tolerance of the same unmodified behavior. This type of tolerance is not virtuous, it's self-destructive. When you forgive a betrayal, your relationship is like a hamster and a wheel. They both go round and round, although nothing changes. To expect your player to change their behavior because you forgave them is to self-sacrifice and make an allowance—the allowance acts as a shield to prevent you from making tough decisions. If you fail to make the tough decision first, you will get hurt. Each time you fail to say, "No more" and allow your player to continue, his lack of respect for your gift of forgiveness will make each subsequent betrayal more painful. Know the game has already ended.

To better understand forgiveness is to let go of attachments. We attach ourselves to our player, our expectations, our disappointments, and our side of the story. Let go. Your happiness is not your player's responsibility. He owes you nothing. Your attachments will be your downfall. When your player makes a hurtful move, you are to acknowledge the behavior without blame or responsibility, accepting that he has free will to choose his move. When you attach yourself to your players move, you are likely to be offended. Allow your player to be autonomous. Accept that his move will either be motivated by love or not love. Your forgiveness is not required. Forgiveness implies an underlining assumption of trust. Most people believe that if you truly forgive without holding a grudge, it's coupled with a renewed sense of trust. This is a false assumption. You may detach from the betrayal, but once the trust is lost, the authentic relationship is over. Test the theory by removing forgiveness from the equation. Do you trust or not trust your player? It's that simple. Letting go of the betrayal is not the issue. Reestablishing trust is near impossible. For this reason, I pray you are motivated to be accountable and committed to your game.

In the end, to forgive your player simply means to let go of blame and playing the victim. You are just as much responsible because you failed to recognize your player. So don't hold a grudge, don't seek revenge, be kind, and continue to be respectful. Although the game is over, it's imperative that you maintain your King because the universe is watching.

CHANCES

By definition, chance is something unexpected, not planned, predicted or controlled. It's a risk. A risk is to give opportunity to an unknown outcome. It's a gamble. In The Game, there are no chances because there is no risk. You have all the instruction you need to be a well-informed, Master player. Whatever move your player decides to make, you've been given the correct move in response. Your move is always love—a virtuous behavior. A risk is a blind spot in your perception. You don't have a blind spot because you've been shown what to look for by the rules, pieces, and Five Gates. The only risk to consider is a business relationship where value must be given before delivery. Be diligent in your observation to minimize the potential loss. -

To not give someone a chance will probably feel contrary to what you've been taught about love and how love behaves. To not give your player a chance certainly doesn't appear to be loving. This instruction is contrary to a common perspective seeming a bit harsh as chances and forgiveness have been touted as integral pieces for a successful relationship. "Nobody is perfect." That's the point. If we are to elevate, we must hold a higher standard for our self-discipline. As long as we make allowances for who and how we are, there will be no incentive to commit to the virtuous character that's required to experience the true power of love. The question now becomes, 'how can forgiveness be a virtue, but I'm not to give chances?' Let's go back to the board. Forgiveness is a pardon you give to yourself, not your player. The virtue is to recognize your own mistakes, avoid the pity party, then forgive yourself and strive to do better. Forgiveness does not apply to your player because you cannot blame or play victim; those are the rules. If there's no one to blame, and you're not a victim, what's left to forgive? The act of forgiveness is meant to help us accept what we cannot change in the lower vibrations of consciousness. The ego struggles to forgive because it blames and feels victimized. Once you elevate your consciousness, you realize that you and your player are both independent with your decisions. The conscious player will acknowledge and accept the move without taking it personally. Consider a simple accident. If player A spills milk, the move for player B is to acknowledge and accept the accident. Move and counter move, one move at a time. There's no need to blame player A for the spilled milk, take the spill personally, make assumptions as to why it was spilled, or make mention about who paid for the milk. The conscious player makes one move to solve the problem.

When you feel inclined to give your player a chance, the translation is, your player has more value than you do. Do you love your player more than you love yourself? To love others before yourself is contrary to the order. Don't confuse chances with mercy. What about children? Loving yourself first is to discipline your behavior before breaking the rules to discipline your child. You must commit to self-mastery first. Your covenant with the Holy Spirit in you is always first priority. Do not give chances to redeem your trust after your player betrays you. Just make certain that you aren't guilty of having unfulfilled expectations or have been offended because of your own insecurities. Self-check before calling it quits. Observing your player to gain confirmation of a lost King is not the same as giving chances. Patient observation helps with your discernment. If the King is lost, acknowledge and accept the move without chances. Don't give your player another opportunity to hurt you. Recognize the betrayal. The Game is over. To continue the relationship will be superficial at best. Further pain is inevitable.

TRUST

The definition of trust is guardianship: a safe keeping for your heart. Each of us is the guardian of our own heart. Proverbs 4:23, "Above all else, guard your heart, for everything flows from it." To guard your heart is to stay in truth, to love in good service. For every thought, word, and behavior flows from your heart, revealing the truth about who you are. Who you are to yourself and others should be trustworthy, affirmed by keeping your King on the board. The challenge is not easy. Your player's trust in you can be lost without you knowing. Stay focused on the board and your virtues so you can stay in play.

Never assume that you have earned your players trust when you've not made enough virtuous moves to prove your character. Even when you know who you are, don't assume your player can see it. If your player prematurely lets his guard down, trusting you to "be himself," it's not to your credit. Any fool is apt to trust you, ignorant to the character he himself is revealing. Should you see this behavior in your player, know that he doesn't have discernment. A lack of discernment equates to having no boundaries. When your player has no boundaries, there's no limit to his destructive behavior. No boundaries, no trust. Game over. When you're able to see the end, there's no reason to play the game. Just be respectful and respectable when you leave the table.

How will you know when to trust your player? It can be in as little as one move. Listen carefully to their response to recognize a rule or a virtue. Did they make an assumption or were they sarcastic? Were they respectful to consider or ask questions? When you've played long enough, you'll learn to recognize very quickly. The player doesn't change, only circumstances. Watch how they react to stressful situations. Anyone can play nice until they're triggered by challenges. How they treat you and others when they're angry is the true test of character. Don't be confused when your player treats different people differently. The weakest link in their behavior is the strength of their character. Your player will either prove his honor by showing you his pieces, or lose it by breaking the rules. If you don't see his virtue now, he'll continue to prove there is none. For this reason, it's imperative that you learn to elevate yourself to a higher standard by making virtuous moves to prove your character. When you learn to place all of your faith and trust in God (love your pieces), your fear of trusting others will no longer be an issue. All of your circumstances can be resolved with one right move. You'll learn the value of trusting your player after you learn how difficult it is to become trustworthy. How do you recognize a life-long player? He is equally yoked in character.

How will you know when the King is lost?

In the beginning, you won't. It happens in an instant when you or your player encounters a betrayal. A slip of the tongue is all it takes: public humiliation, condemnation, condescendence, bullying, sarcasm, demeaning, and avoidance, all hurt. When you've lost your King, and your player loses his trust in you, his energy will shift. He will become distant, reluctant to spend time or converse with you. He won't laugh at your jokes. He won't offer his service to help you. He won't edify you or connect you to others. Your spouse will be less affectionate and less inspired to experience new things with you. You'll be passed over for promotions and left out of social invitations. Your opinion won't be respected, nor will your knowledge be requested. Conversations will be short and uninteresting, leaving your relationships in a shallow existence. When you lose your King, your life becomes glaringly loveless.

Never *expect* your player to have a "thick skin," ready to forgive your indiscretions. He may let the broken rule slide, but the crack you create will continue to grow wider into a divide too distant to recover. Be responsible to increase your self-awareness about how you sound in your communication. For example, to acknowledge and accept, you wouldn't say, "I know, you said that a million times already." This response is disrespectful and pushes love away. The proper response would be, "How can I make this better?" The question acknowledges your player's move without insult. Take the high road. You are responsible for your standard of communication. If you make excuses for your hurtful words, you lower your vibration to the point of self-sabotage because words have power. Watch your words to see God's favor manifest.

How will you know if your player trusts you? Make a commitment to think, speak, and behave in virtue. When you do, you'll experience your player's Respect, by his edification and loyalty toward you. If your King is firmly on the board, your player will recognize you. Your honor and integrity will be apparent. When the universe sees your loving behavior others will see it too.

How do you know you can trust God? How do you know you can't? The only way to know is to commit to love, then experience the evidence. God wants you to fulfill the law. Romans 13:8 says; "Let no debt remain outstanding, except the continuing debt to love one another, for he who loves his fellow man has fulfilled the law." When you fulfill the law, God delivers. When you don't know how to consistently fulfill the law, favor is brushed off as coincidence. If you want consistent results, you must be consistently loving.

What is God's promise? Psalms 91:9-11, "If you say, The Lord is my refuge, and make the Most High your dwelling, no harm will overtake you, no disaster will come near your tent. For he will command his angels concerning you to guard you in all your ways." Who has the power and authority to make such a claim over your life? Only God can deliver this promise.

Why should you put all of your faith and trust in God? There is nothing greater, more powerful, or more reliable than the unseen field of pure potential. Money and accounting will never deliver supernatural protection. God (love) is proven by science. An infallible, omnipotent existence.

> *God is Love.*
> *Love is Energy.*
> *Energy is an Existence.*
> *Existence is Everything, and,*
> *Everything is God.*
>
> ~Princess Merrilee of Solana

God is all there is. There is nothing else. If not God what is it? Our perception of division between the seen and unseen is our limiting belief. Energy will never fail to exist. The presence of the Holy Spirit energy is in you. Which is why you can't escape The Game. This energy is responsive to every thought, word, and feeling of what you are. Playing The Game will elevate you to your most amazing life experience as a purposefully loving creator. This magical substance of God in you is real, and it follows the law to the letter.

When you trust your player before you're certain of their character, know that your heart is searching for a way home to love, but the ego redirects your pure intention, leading you to heartbreak again. With the application of The Game, your virtues will give you clarity to prevent you from the misfortune of heartbreak as you become confident in your perception of unloving behavior.

Aim to eliminate the ego to become perfect with the Spirit of love. The result is Holy matrimony. Holy matrimony is the marriage bed. You are married to God. One with love. Your heart will be fulfilled without the need for another. When two experience one in Holy matrimony with God, they are now prepared to become one flesh. Equally yoked. A match made in heaven.

$Part\ 26$

MOVING YOUR PIECES

LET'S PUT IT ALL TOGETHER

In The Game, there is no strategy, manipulation, or premeditated moves. There is only love with each present move.

The next virtuous move is all you need to know in response to your players move. Whether it be a test from the universe, a direct move by your player, or a personal dilemma, the only information you need to stay at the highest vibration is how to move the one correct piece right now. Fearful "what if" rumination is an illusion until realized. One move at a time is how you eliminate worry. Make the right move right now and have faith that the universe will direct circumstances in your favor. You have access to all the answers to solve any situation, problem, dilemma, and desire when you use all of your pieces on your board. There is nothing more. There is nothing hidden or left out. Everything you need to secure your happiness is within those pieces. Your board has the power to remedy any fearful or tough situation in your life. The formula never fails.

Now it's time to put it all together. Your success is imminent when you remember the purpose of The Game. Be one with the Most High vibration—love, (God, universe, and creator. Whatever reference you choose, remember all is God. There is nothing else)—so that you and those of your concern will be supernaturally protected and you will live your life in favor. When you master your responses, you master The Game of life. Back to the garden where everything is provided. You become the way, the truth and the life. No power is greater. The Game is simple, but it's not easy. Learning to substitute old behaviors (rules) for your new virtues (pieces) brings the greatest reward, more than you can ever imagine.

Keep these points in the forefront of your mind. Slow down and think. To stay in play, you must be honorable. Period.

- Aim for a lifelong relationship. Don't try to control your player. Self-discipline wins the game.

- Faith and patience combined are one move.

- Pause. Let your player lead, you respond.

- One move is often a combination of virtues.

- Do not interrupt your players move. Pause. Be patient and wait for your turn.

- Don't hesitate to sacrifice your pride to maintain your honor.

- Know the Five Gates. She may be beautiful in appearance, sexy in personality, and highly intelligent, but without a virtuous character, you will get hurt.

- **One player at a time, multiple boards.** Think about how your move will affect your relationship with your player and how the universe will notify your spectators.

- **When you don't know the answer, it's not time to move.** Wait in faith knowing your answer is on the way.

- Patience is to let go. Detach from your need to control the outcome.

- **Your Honor, Faith, and Patience work together. Like a dance, One…two…three…**all in unified silence.

- One…two…three…and **move four** is to **Acknowledge and Accept.** A simple, "Okay, then what?" will keep the conversation flowing. Pause.

- Remain patient and be humble to **let the game play out.** Let your player lead even when you think you know where you're headed.

- Add a little **Humor.**

- **When in doubt, ask a question.** Never assume. Get confirmation.

- Your next moves require discernment based on the content of the conversation.

- One…two…three…and four are the first moves.

- The other virtues will depend on your situation. **You can use One, two, three and four many times over without having to use a different piece.**

- The next move will incorporate Compassion, Contribution, or Charity. How can I help?

- You will learn how to **combine your pieces to make one move** as you go.

- **Acknowledge and Accept is the first spoken move before adding another.**

- Acknowledge and Accept, be Respectable and Edify. Your King is firmly on the board.

- **Acknowledge and Accept, be Respectful with Grace.** Get to know your player.

- The further along in the game, you'll begin to notice your player breaking the rules.

- **Game over is a loss of trust.** But walking away must **wait until you have firm evidence of betrayal—an obvious display of disrespect. Not a lack of respect. Know the difference.**

- Keep a light and friendly disposition. There's no need to protect yourself with a grim attitude or guarded body language. You have the armor of your pieces. Be confident.

- **Acknowledge and accept, resilience, and faith.** Accept your mistake. Dust yourself off and keep going.

- **Acknowledge and accept, forgiveness, compassion, and self-awareness.** Forgive yourself. Be kind and be aware to correct your behavior.

- **Acknowledge and Accept, Mercy, Grace.** People aren't perfect. Be kind. Say something nice.

- **Faith, Patience, Loyalty.** Believe in the best. Wait. Be loyal to your commitment to love.

- **Patience, Tolerance, Gratitude.** Let go of the need for control. Detach from your player. Be thankful that you know how to love better by virtuous behavior.

- **Humility, Resilience, Grace.** Take it on the chin. Don't give up. Hold your tongue if you can't be nice.

- **Diplomacy and Humor.** Never make your player the bud of a joke. Poke fun but don't be sarcastic with your player.

- **Patience, Nobility, and Wisdom.** Most people don't have self-awareness. Watch yourself, step up and take responsibility to do the right thing. Do not take credit for your noble behavior.

- **Patience and Humor.** Let go of controlling behavior to find the humor with your children.

- **Respect, Mercy, and Grace.** Be respectable to earn respect, extend favor where not deserved and deliver with a kind word.

- **Integrity, Loyalty, and Wisdom.** Keep your word. Keep his confidence. Know the importance.

- **Respect, Edify, remain Loyal.** Lift up your player. Speak good about him. Don't betray his trust in you.

The examples above are to show you how to use all of your pieces interchangeably. You won't have all the pieces when you begin. You may not even have a King. Self-awareness followed by self-discipline will get you moving in the right direction. Be patient, it's not easy.

As you learn to use your pieces, know that you don't need to try to convince your player of your value. You don't need to over explain the contemplation going on in your head. You don't need to prove your intelligence or share your side of the story. You don't need to be right or defend yourself against accusations. You don't need permission. And you don't need to explain your reasoning for game over. Much of being virtuous is having diplomacy and discernment with the information you share. Be transparent but don't be victim to an interrogation.

Part 27

GAME OVER

The idea of "Game Over" may seem unrealistic as you struggle to understand how to be so callous. How are you to walk away so easily? If you can't forgive others for their mistakes, how can you expect to be forgiven for yours? This is exactly the point. Which is why you'll grow to appreciate The Game. Raising your standards will help you to walk away from unhealthy relationships where you've been wasting your time. No more self-sacrifice. You are becoming a Master player. You deserve equally yoked loving relationships.

Once you start playing, it won't take long for you to realize that you don't trust very many people in your circle. That discovery will hurt. Game Over is a very harsh reality to escape when you realize how alone you are. But once you realize when the game is over, it will become increasingly more difficult for you to continue any superficial relationship. Remember, game over is a loss of trust evidenced by their unloving behavior. Betrayal is a dishonorable act against you. Whether too many broken rules or betrayal, a loss of trust is the time you walk away. Game Over means there's no King, no respect, no love. In either case, the divide is too distant to bring the relationship back to whole. Without knowing why, you'll accept that you just grew apart. In reality, the respect was lost, and somebody missed it.

Moving away from the table can be figurative or literal. In either case, it means you're no longer in play with your player. Most of the time you won't need to physically remove yourself from the presence of your player, but mentally you know they are not worthy of your time investment any longer. The last and final move is to acknowledge and accept their move with grace. Use simple words or nothing at all. Don't give them your energy by explaining your reasoning. To do so will keep you in play as your player has been granted a "chance" to recover. The implication says you are willing to forgive and keep playing. You don't want to lead your player to believe you're still in play. Stop talking. If you're going to go higher, you must pass these very crucial tests. The more difficult the test, the bigger the reward. The test creates an opportunity for you to win favor when your thinking is correct. You control your response, not your player. The more virtuous your response, the more amazing the favor. The universal law of cause and effect.

As you begin to master The Game, the value of "Game Over" becomes your superpower. You'll no longer waste time and energy trusting people who don't have a King on the board. The sooner you recognize the missing piece, the less time and energy you'll invest in relationships not worthy of your effort. Eventually, you will recognize game over in just one move. Walking away will never be an issue.

THE CONCLUSION OF THE MATTER

Applying the complexity of The Game in its entirety will be uncomfortable at first, but it pales in comparison to the reality of wasting your life ignorant to the answer. Self-discipline takes time, attention, and a commitment to your best-self. Self-mastery demands an intimate relationship with yourself *above all else.* When you love yourself enough to want the delivery of your gift, you become a super power for others to follow. You can pull the sword from the stone and fear nothing—not tomorrow, not illness, not poverty or misfortune. With the full armor of God you will never be forsaken. Love yourself enough to commit to God's promise and your value will never be mistaken.

WELCOME HOME

You now hold the key to the Kingdom.

There is no going back, your journey has begun.

The change is taking place even before reaching the end of this instruction.

You have activated the call to Christ consciousness.

The universe is watching and your angels are waiting to deliver your favor.

All you have to do is make the right move.

"To the one who is victorious and does my will to the end,
I will give authority over the nations."

Revelation 2:26

"I no longer call you servants because the servant does not
know his master's business. Instead, I call you friends, for every-
thing I learn from my Father I have made known to you."

John 15:15

ACKNOWLEDGMENTS

To my mother, Josephine Klein, you were right. I Let go and Let God.

To my children: Samuel, Peter, Benjamin, and Emma, thank you for inspiring me to become love. Listen to your grandmother.

To my children's father, Douglas M. Sweeney Jr., to whom without these words may never have been written. Thank you for placing all of your faith and trust in God.

HRM Princess Merrilee of Solana®©™

One of the purest abstracts of humanity and kindness embodied in a woman of goodwill and faith, unwavering in her standing, graceful in her vision, and above all else, proof positive that love is the answer.

k/w King's Minister for The Kingdom of Terathea and Testamentary Executor for The State of Grace. Grace, NA 2020 Ag-ASST